The Economic Organization

WITH AN ARTICLE
NOTES ON UTILITY AND COST

FRANK H. KNIGHT

Martino Fine Books
Eastford, CT
2017

Martino Fine Books
P.O. Box 913,
Eastford, CT 06242 USA

ISBN 978-1-68422-072-4

Copyright 2017
Martino Fine Books

Cover Design Tiziana Matarazzo

Printed in the United States of America On 100% Acid-Free Paper

The Economic Organization

WITH AN ARTICLE
NOTES ON UTILITY AND COST

FRANK H. KNIGHT

AUGUSTUS M. KELLEY
New York
1951

TABLE OF CONTENTS

Social Economic Organization

It is somewhat unusual to begin the treatment of a subject with a warning against attaching too much importance to it; but in the case of economics, such an injunction is quite as much needed as explanation and emphasis of the importance it really has. It is characteristic of the age in which we live to think too much in terms of economics, to see things too predominantly in their economic aspect; and this is especially true of the American people. There is no more important prerequisite to clear thinking in regard to economics itself than is recognition of its limited place among human interests at large.

COMMON DEFINITIONS OF ECONOMICS MUCH TOO BROAD, THOUGH THE ECONOMIC CONCEPTION OF LIFE IS TOO NARROW. In modern usage, the term economic has come to be used in a sense which is practically synonymous with intelligent or rational. This is the first and broadest conception of the term, within which we have to find by narrowing it down progressively, a definition which will describe the actual subject-matter of the science of political economy. It is in accord with good linguistic usage to think and speak of the whole problem of living as one of economy, the economical use of time, energy, etc.—*resource* of every sort. Many definitions of economics found in text books fall into this error of including virtually all intelligent behavior. One writer has actually given as his definition of economics the "science of rational activity." Others find its subject matter is "man's activity in making a living", or "the ordinary business of life". Such definitions come too near to saying that economics is the science of things generally, of everything that men are for practical reasons interested in. Such a definition is useless and misleading. It is necessary to devote a little time to making clear the restrictions which mark off the modestly limited domain of economic science within the inclusive sphere of knowledge as a whole.

In the first place, it should be understood that economizing, even in this broad sense of rational activity, or the intelligent use of given means in achieving given ends, does not include all human interests, and that the kind of knowledge on which such activity rests does not exhaust the field of human knowledge. It is, as we have said, one of the errors, not to say vices, of an age in which the progress of natural science and the triumphs of its application to life have engrossed men's attention, to look upon life too exclusively under this aspect of scientific rationality. It is requisite to a proper orientation to economic science itself as well as necessary to a sound philosophy of life, to see clearly that life must be more than economics, or rational conduct, or the intelligent accurate manipulation of materials and use of power in achieving results. Such a view is too narrow. It implies that the results to be achieved are to be taken for granted, whereas in fact the results themselves are often quite as much in question as the means and procedures for achieving results. Living intelligently includes more than the intelligent use of means in realizing ends; it is fully as important to select the ends intelligently, for intelligent action directed toward wrong ends only makes evil greater and more certain. One must have intelligent tastes, and intelligent opinions on many things which do not directly relate to conduct at all. Not only are the objectives of action in fact a practical problem, as well as the means of achievement, but intelligent discussion of the means cannot be separated from the discussion of the ends.

Living is an art: and art is more than a matter of a scientific technique, and the richness and value of life are largely bound up in the "more". In its reaction from the futility of medievalism and mystical speculation, the modern Western world has gone far to the other extreme. It loses much of the value of life through neglect of the imponderables and incommensurables, and gets into a false conception of the character of social and individual problems. Our thinking about life-values runs too much in terms of material prerequisites and costs. It is an exaggeration which may be useful to say that economic goods as a class are predominantly "necessary" rather than truly valuable. The importance of economic provision is chiefly that of a prerequisite to the enjoyment of the free goods of the world, the beauty of the natural scene, the intercourse of friends in "aimless" camaraderie, the appreciation and creation of art, discovery of truth and communion with one's own inner being and the Nature of Things. Civilization should look forward to a day when the material product of industrial activity shall become rather its by-product, and its primary significance shall be that of a sphere for creative self-expression and the development of a higher type of individual and of human fellowship. It ought to be the first aim of economic policy to reduce the importance of economic policy in life as a whole. So it ought to be the highest objective in the study of economics to hasten the day when the study and the practice of economy will recede into the background of men's thoughts, when food and shelter, and all provision for physical needs, can be taken for granted without serious thought, when "production" and "consumption" and "distribution" shall cease from troubling and pass below the threshold of consciousness and the effort and planning of the mass of mankind may be mainly devoted to problems of beauty, truth, right human relations and cultural growth.

THE ACTUAL SUBJECT MATTER OF ECONOMICS. What is discussed in the science of economics includes a relatively small fraction of the economic side of life taken in the broad sense. It has nothing to do with the concrete processes of producing or distributing goods, or using goods to satisfy wants. The study of these matters comes under the head of technology, including engineering, business management, and home economics. Economics deals with the *social organization* of economic activity. In practice its scope is much narrower still; there are many ways in which economic activity may be socially organized, but the predominant method in modern nations is the price system, or free enterprise. Consequently it is the structure and working of the system of free enterprise which constitutes the principal topic of discussion in a treatise on economics.

THE MEANING OF ORGANIZATION. Everyone is familiar with the idea of division of labor—by which is really meant specialization of labor—and many economists have taken it as their point of departure in expounding the science of economics. This was the procedure of Adam Smith, for example, whose book, *The Wealth of Nations*, published in the year 1776, ranks as the first modern treatise on economics.

Modern economic society is often compared with a living body or "organism" and the comparison is certainly suggestive. The essential similarity and the fundamental idea for our purpose is precisely that of division of labor or specialization. But the expression "division" of labor, does not tell us enough. The idea is rather division into different *kinds* of labor. A number of men hoeing in a field or nailing shingles on a roof exemplify "division" of labor, but not organization. The problems of organization arise only when *different things are being done*, in the furtherance of a *common end*, and in definite relations to each other, i.e., in *coordination*. A single man in raising a crop or building a house shows division of labor in another sense, since he does many different things, but this is not yet organization in the sense with which we are concerned. The human body shows organization in the true sense, since the various "organs" not only perform different functions, but must all act in a substantially continuous manner and in proper adjustment to each other. Again, organization must be distinguished from cooperation; it involves cooperation, but more. If a group of men lift a stone which is too heavy for one to move alone, they cooperate, and increase their power by cooperation; their action is cooperative, but they are not organized, since they are all doing the same thing.

It is obvious enough that the economic or living-making activities of the modern world are very elaborately organized. We need not pause to comment on the number of persons who have contributed, and in what different ways, in supplying the wants of the humblest citizen today. The authorities of the federal census prepare a catalogue or classification of occupations which lists many thousands of these economic functions for the working population of the United States alone and which yet makes no pretense of distinguishing all specialized functions. For instance, farm laborers are classed together though different individuals work at the production of a wide variety of crops. It is evident also that the accomplishment of the ultimate purpose of it all, the provision for the needs and desires of the people, depends upon these various operations being carried on with a fair degree of continuity and tolerable coordination. The problem of organization, which sets the problem of economic science, deals with the concrete means or mechanism for dividing the general function of making a living for the people into parts and bringing about the performance of these parts in due proportion and harmony.

More specifically, it is a problem of the social machinery for accomplishing *five fairly distinct functions.* Every system of organization must perform these tasks, and it is its success or failure in discharging these functions which determines its value as a system. Back of the study of economics is the practical need of making the organization better, and we can hope for success in this task only if we proceed to it intelligently, which is to say on the basis of an understanding of the nature of the work which a system of organization has to perform, and of the alternatives open in the way of possible types of organization machinery.

The Five Main Functions of an Economic System

The general task of organizing the economic activity of society may be divided into a number of fundamental functions. These are in fact very much inter-connected

7

and overlapping, but the distinction is useful as an aid to discussing the existing economic order both descriptively and critically, its structure as well as its workings. These functions fall into a more or less logical sequence. The first is to decide what is to be done, that is, what goods and services are to be produced, and in what proportions. It is the function of setting standards, of establishing a social scale of values, or the function of social choice; the second is the function of organizing production, in the narrow sense, of getting done the things settled upon as most worth doing; third is distribution, the apportioning of the product among the members of society; the fourth is really a group of functions having to do with maintaining and improving the social structure, or promoting social progress.

1. THE FUNCTION OF FIXING STANDARDS; THE NOTION OF EFFICIENCY. In a world where organizations were absent, where each individual carried on his life activities in isolation and independence of all others, the matter of standards would be simply a matter of individual choice. But when the production of wealth is socialized, there has to be a *social* decision as to the relative importance of different uses of productive power, as to which wants are to be satisfied and which left unsatisfied or to what extent any one is to be satisfied at the expense of any other. In the case of an individual, choice need be made only among his own wants; but in a social system, the wants of different individuals also come into conflict. As far as this is a quantitative question merely, of how far the wants of one are to be gratified at the expense of the wants of another, or left ungratified in favor of another, the problem is one of *distribution,* and will be noticed under another heading (the third function). But to a large and increasing extent, society finds it necessary or advisable further to regulate the individual's regulation of his own want-satisfaction, to enforce a community standard of living. As a matter of fact, these two problems are closely interlaced, the question of *whose* wants and that of *which* wants are to be given preference, and in what measure. It is important to observe that they are

largely the same question. The difference in the "amount" consumed by different persons is not mainly a difference in the amounts of the same commodities; different persons consume different things, which are quantitatively compared only through the agency of the value scale itself. Nevertheless there seems to be ample justification for a logical separation of the questions of what is to be produced from that of who is to get the product, and for discussing separately the relations between the two phases of organization.

A point of fundamental importance in connection with the question of standards is that of the origin or ultimate source of wants. The system of social organization does more than reduce individual values to a common denominator or scale of equivalence. In large part the individual wants themselves are *created* by social intercourse, and their character is also largely dependent upon the form of organization of the economic system upon which they are dependent for their gratification. The workings of the economic organization in this connection form a problem too large and complex to be discussed at any length in a small book like this one. Indeed, the subject of wants is not only vast in scope but apparently cannot be reduced to scientific terms, except within rather narrow limits, falling rather in the field of art. The scientific discussion of economics has to be restricted in the main to the analysis of the organization of want-satisfaction. In the science of economics the wants are largely taken for granted as facts of the time and place, and the discussion of their origin and formation is left for the most part to the distinct studies of social psychology and cultural anthropology.[1]

The problem of standards or values occupies a key position in Economics. The practical objective of economics, it must be kept in mind, is that of improving the social organization and increasing its efficiency. There is a com-

[1] The deliberate creation or changing of wants for specific commodities as by advertising, is to some extent an exception, but in the main such activities must be regarded as creating a *knowledge of* certain *means* of satisfying wants rather than as changing ultimate *wants*.

mon misconception that it is possible to measure or discuss efficiency in purely physical terms. The first principles of physics or engineering science teach that this is not true, that the term efficiency involves the idea of value, and some measure of value as well. It is perhaps the most important principle of physical science that neither matter nor energy can be created or destroyed, that whatever goes into any process must come out in some form, and hence as a mere matter of physical quantity, the efficiency of all operations would equal one hundred per cent. The correct definition of efficiency is the ratio, not between "output" and "input" but between *useful* output and total output or input. Hence efficiency, even in the simplest energy transformation, is meaningless without a measure of usefulness or value. In any attempt to understand economic efficiency, the notion of value is more obviously crucial since most economic problems are concerned with a number of kinds both of outlay and of return, and there is no conceivable way of making comparisons without first reducing all the factors to terms of a common measure. It will appear in due course that the science of economics is largely taken up with description and analysis of the process by which this common denominator of things consumed and produced by the economic system is arrived at, that is, with the *problem of measuring values.*

2. THE FUNCTION OF ORGANIZING PRODUCTION. The second step, logically speaking, after the ranking and grading of the uses to which productive power may be put, is that of actually putting them to use in accordance with the scale of values thus established. From a social point of view, this process may be viewed under two aspects, (a) the assignment or *allocation* of the available productive forces and materials among the various lines of industry, and (b) the effective *coordination* of the various means of production in each industry into such groupings as will produce the greatest result. The second of these tasks properly belongs to technological rather than to economic science, and is treated in economics only with reference to the interrelations between the organiza-

tion of society as a whole and the internal organization ot
the industries.

3. THE FUNCTION OF DISTRIBUTION. This third function
would not exist at all in an unorganized world. Each individual, acting independently of all others, would simply
consume what he produced. But where production is socialized, the separate productive contribution of one par-
ticipant in the process cannot be directly identified or
separated. It is apparent that a modern factory operative,
say one who spends all his time putting buttons on shoes
or nailing the covers on packing cases, cannot live on his
own product, physically interpreted. When we further
consider that different individuals contribute to production in fundamentally different ways, many by furnishing
land or other "natural resources" or material equipment
or money or managerial or supervisory services, or by selling goods, and in other ways which make no identifiable
physical change in any product, it is manifest that if everyone is to get a living out of the process some *social
mechanism* of distribution is called for.

In this connection should be recalled the close relation
between distribution and the control of production. The
decision as to what to produce is closely bound up with
the decision for whom to produce. There is also a close
relation between the third function and the second. In
our social system distribution is the chief agency relied
upon to control production and stimulate efficiency. Ours
is a system of "private property", "free competition" and
"contract". This means that every productive resource or
agent, including labor power, typically "belongs" to some
person who is free within the legal conditions of marketing, to get what he can out of its use. It is assumed, and
the course of the argument will show at length why it is
true, that there is in some effective sense a real positive
connection between the productive contribution made by
any productive agent and the remuneration which its
"owner" can secure for its use. Hence this remuneration
(a distributive share) and the wish to make it as large as
possible, constitute the chief reliance of society for an in-

centive to place the agency into use in the general productive system in such a way as to make it as productive as possible. The strongest argument in favor of such a system as ours is the contention that this direct, selfish motive is the only dependable method, or at least the best method, for guaranteeing that productive forces will be organized and worked efficiently. The argument assumes that in spite of the difficulty above referred to of identifying the particular contribution to the social product made by any person or piece of property, it is possible to separate it out, and measure it, in terms of value and that the distributive system does this with accuracy enough to make remunerations vary in accord with product. If this were not true in the main, remuneration could not really afford an incentive to productive efficiency, and an economic order based on individualism would not function.

4. ECONOMIC MAINTENANCE AND PROGRESS. There is no moral connotation in the term progress; it refers to any persistent cumulative change, whether regarded as good or bad. The principal forms of economic progress include, (1) growth of population and any cumulative change in its composition or education which affects either its productive powers or its wants; (2) the accumulation of material aids to production or "capital" of all kinds, including such permanent sources of satisfaction as newly discovered natural resources and also works of art; [2] (3) improvements in technical processes or changes in the form of business organization. It is to be noted especially that progress has two sorts of significance for the economic organization. First, it is one of the products or values created by the latter, at a cost; i.e., it involves using productive power for this purpose and sacrificing its use for other purposes; and second, it affects and changes the character of the economic system itself and the conditions under which the system works.

This fourth function of organization, especially the provision for progress, cuts across all the other three. It is

[2] Destruction and exhaustion of resources not replaced is also a progressive change.

Social Economic Organization

a matter of standards or values to decide how much progress society can afford or cares to have at the cost of sacrificing present values, and what forms it shall take; it is a matter of productive organization to utilize the determined share of available productive power to bring about progress in the amount and of the kinds decided upon, and it is a problem of distribution to apportion the burdens and benefits of progress among the members of society. We may be reminded also that it is true of progress as of all other lines of human action that it comes within the field of economics just in so far as it is related to the organized system of producing and distributing the means of want-satisfaction.

The first three of these functions (or four, since No. 2 is really double, involving two aspects) are relatively "short-time" in character. They are all aspects of the general problem of an economic society working under "given conditions", in contrast with the fourth function which relates to the problem of improving the given conditions through the course of time. The first three therefore make up the problems of what may be called the "stationary economy". If society either could not or did not try to grow and progress and make improvements, its economic problem would be entirely within this field. But since economic societies do in fact face problems of growth and improvement, and make some effort to solve them intelligently, we have to add the fourth function, or group of functions. Such problems are frequently referred to under the head of "dynamic" economics; for reasons which cannot be given in detail here, this is a seriously misleading use of language, and they should be called simply problems of progress or historical problems.

The "given conditions" of the stationary economy are included under the three heads of *resources, wants,* and *technology,* which may be subdivided and classified in more elaborate ways. The separation is based on the plain and simple fact that with reference to social calculations and plans which look ahead only a few years, these factors, resources, wants and the technological system will not change enough to affect the argument or plans seri-

13

ously. But looking ahead over historical time they do change, to an indefinite extent, and the production and guidance of changes in them becomes the dominant character of the social economic problem. In the "short-run" (of a few years), however, the problem is to utilize in the best way the existing resources and technology in the satisfaction of existing wants.

A FIFTH FUNCTION: TO ADJUST CONSUMPTION TO PRODUCTION WITHIN VERY SHORT PERIODS. For completeness, this survey of functions should point out that within *very short* periods society faces still another set of "given conditions", hence still another type of problem, and in consequence its economic organization has still another task or function to perform, though this fifth function is rarely distinguished sharply from those of the "stationary economy" point of view. From this latter point of view, the problem is to adjust production to consumption under the given conditions. But in many cases, production cannot be adjusted quickly, while demand conditions do change rapidly; and in addition, production in many fields is subject to fluctuations from causes beyond control. In consequence, the supply of many commodities is fixed for considerable periods of time, on a level more or less divergent from the best possible adjustment to existing conditions of demand. The supply on hand is of course the result of productive operations in the past, and has to suffice until it can be changed. In agriculture this is conspicuously true. The crop of a given year has to last until the next year's crop is produced (except in so far as other parts of the world having different crop seasons can be drawn upon). In the case of manufactured goods, production is not definitely periodic, but it is still true that the rate of production frequently cannot be changed in a short time, to meet changes in demand, at least not without enormous cost.

It follows that over short periods consumption has to be controlled and distributed with reference to an existing supply or current rate of production, at the same time that adjustment of production to consumption requirements is being made as rapidly as practicable. The existing supply of wheat or potatoes, for example, must be distributed (a) over the season for which it has to suffice and (b) among the different consumers and their different needs. Thus there is a fifth function of organization, the opposite in a sense, of number two in the four above discussed, namely the short-run adjustment of consumption to past or current production.[3]

Advantages and Disadvantages of Organized Action

THE REASONS FOR ORGANIZING ACTIVITY. As previously remarked, a high degree of organization in human activity is a fairly recent development in the world's history, and is still restricted mainly to what we call the European peoples or cultures. The urge behind its development can be stated in the single word *efficiency*. The object of industrial activity is to utilize an available fund of productive agencies and resources in making the goods and services with which people satisfy their wants. Organized effort enables a social group to produce more of the means of want-satisfaction than it could by working as individuals. During the course of history, the possibility of increased efficiency has led to an ever greater degree of specialization, which in turn has constantly called for a more elaborate and effective mechanism of coordination and control, just as the higher animals require an enormously more complex nervous and circulatory system than the lower. It will be worth while to carry the analysis a little beyond the general notion of efficiency and see some of the reasons why specialized effort yields larger or better results. We must then turn to the other side of the picture and note some of the disadvantages of organization.

[3] It is rather typical of economic phenomena that cause and effect relations are apt to run in opposite directions in the short-run and the long-run. This is a common source of difficulty in the reasoning, as will appear more fully in the treatment of the forces which fix prices.

The Economic Organization

THE GAINS FROM SPECIALIZATION.[4] The largest gain which the higher animals secure in comparison with lower, less organized forms, arises from the adaptation of structure to function. In the most primitive animals the same kind of tissue has to perform all the divergent functions of locomotion, seizing and ingestion of food, digestion, assimilation, excretion of waste and reproduction, while in the mammalian body the specialization of tissues and organs for the various functions and the increased efficiency with which all are consequently performed, are too evident to need extended comment. Some social insects produce physically divergent types of individuals adapted by structure to perform different functions. In the familiar case of the bees, the bulk of the community is made up of "workers" and the reproductive function is specialized in the queens and drones. Certain species of ants and termites present a very complex social structure containing a dozen or more structurally specialized types of individuals. One of the most interesting facts in regard to human society is the absence of definite structural specialization of individuals. Human organization is an artificial thing, a culture product. Natural differences undoubtedly exist among human beings, and are taken advantage of, more or less, in fitting individuals to specialized functions; but the differences seem to be accidental, and unpredictable. Certainly human beings do not become fused into a superorganism in the manner of the cells in an animal body. It is in fact a matter of the greatest uncertainty and one of the most disputed questions in the whole field of knowledge, as to how far observed differences in kinds and degrees of capacity are innate and how far they are the result of "nurture" and the subtle influences of environment and social suggestion. The tendency of scientific study at the present time is to place more and more emphasis on the environment and less upon congenital structure. In any case, human differences are not so definitely

[4] It will be recalled that we are using the word "specialization" instead of the familiar "division of labor", not only is labor divided, but it is differentiated and co-ordinated, and the other elements or factors in production are likewise "specialized"— often more extensively and vitally than the human factor.

transmitted by inheritance as to be predictable in advance; they have to be discovered and developed and the individual fitted to his place in the system by some artificial means. There is no mechanical solution of the human social problem, as in the case of the animal organism or even of insect societies; human beings have to form themselves into an organization as well as to control and operate it when constructed.

1. UTILIZATION OF NATURAL APTITUDES; ESPECIALLY THOSE OF LEADERS AND FOLLOWERS.   However, we are safe in asserting that there are some innate individual differences in human capacities and aptitudes, and the first in the list of gains from organization results from taking advantage of them. One social problem is to discover such differences and utilize them as far as possible. They can never be predicted with any certainty before the birth of the individual, in fact they cannot usually be discerned at any time in life from clear external marks; and in the course of the development of the individual they become so largely overlaid with acquired traits that they can never be separated from the latter. The most important natural differences of which we can be reasonably sure are those of physical stature and dexterity and (with much less certainty) of general mental activity. The most important differentiation in function, or division of labor, between individuals is the separation between direction and execution, or the specialization of *leadership*. It may well be true that able leaders are in general also more competent workers or operatives, but the gain from superior direction is so much more important than that from superior concrete performance that undoubtedly the largest single source of the increased efficiency through organization results from having work planned and directed by the exceptionally capable individuals, while the mass of the people follow instructions.

2. DEVELOPMENT AND UTILIZATION OF ACQUIRED SKILL AND ACQUIRED KNOWLEDGE.   The principal quality in man which gives him superiority over the animals is his ability to learn, including learning to know and learning to

do. But even in man this capacity is exceedingly limited in scope in comparison with the whole range of acquired human knowledge and activity, and a large part of the gain from organizing activity comes from the increase in the efficiency of learning which is connected with reducing the field in which an individual must exercise his learning ability. Even the specialization of leadership undoubtedly rests as much upon acquired as upon innate differences. In truth, the fundamental innate difference among men is in the capacity to learn itself. In other fields than leadership—fields of specialized knowledge and skill in the narrower sense—it is still more clearly impossible to separate the factor of innate capacity from that of acquired powers, and still more evident that the innate capacity itself is a capacity to learn rather than directly to perform. Even in the case of genius, what is inherited is an extraordinary capacity to learn, or learn to do, certain things, and the amount of actual specialization in the original bent is highly uncertain. In modern machine industry, where the operative is restricted to repetition of a few simple movements, an incredible increase of speed as compared with that of an untrained worker may be achieved in a short space of time. The operations generally involve movements very different from any which are natural to man as an animal, movements such as setting type, playing a musical instrument, or sorting mail matter into boxes; but they can be learned by any normal person, and when mastered they make possible the employment of a technology vastly more efficient than that of primitive industry. (See No. 5 below.)

3. CHANGING PIECES OF WORK CHEAPER, WITHIN LIMITS, THAN CHANGING JOBS. The saving of time and effort in changing from one operation to another is the third gain from specialization. It is true that if a man performs the same operation repeatedly, he must change from one object, or piece of work, to another. But by the use of mechanical conveyers, scientific routing and the like, it is found that, *within limits,* the process of bringing to the workman a procession of shoes, automobile cylinders, or hog carcasses is far less costly than having him make the

changes in position, changes in tools used, etc., involved in performing successively on any one of them the various operations necessary to complete the making of a product, as was done under old handicraft conditions. This gain is evidently rather closely connected with that arising from specialized skill. It is to be especially emphasized, because so commonly overlooked, that in this connection there are offsetting costs, which only within limits are exceeded by the gains. Not only must the cost of changing jobs be compared with the cost of changing pieces of work as within a given factory. If each man completed a product, the workers would not have to be brought together into factories at all, a feature which also involves large costs, and neither would the materials have to be assembled from such a vast area or the product distributed back over a market perhaps nation-wide or even world-wide in extent. The costs of bringing together vast quantities of materials and of distributing the product tend in fact to offset very considerably the gains of large scale production. These costs include not merely actual transportation, but marketing costs in the form of profits, risks and losses from inaccurate forecasting of demand, idleness due to over-production, storage, insurance and the like. The public has been educated by apologists for monopoly to over-estimate seriously the real gains from large-scale factory methods; these offsetting losses are rarely appreciated to the full.

4. NATURAL ADVANTAGES IN THE CASE OF "NATURAL RESOURCES." However uncertain we may be as to the innate differences in men, there can be no question that the natural resources of different regions are suited to widely divergent employments. In such extreme cases as mineral deposits, for example, specialization to regions is absolute, since minerals can only be extracted where they exist, and this is quite commonly in places where any other industry is virtually out of the question. Also, "geographical" or "territorial" specialization is almost a physical necessity as between different climatic zones. Other industries may be carried on in different regions, but usually some locations offer greater or lesser advantages over

others, which may or may not be sufficient to offset transportation costs and other costs of specialization. The question of political interference with territorial specialization, through "tariffs", bounties, subsidies and the like, has formed an important political issue in all modern nations. Such measures practically always reduce the gains from specialization and the arguments used to support them are fallacious from a purely economic point of view. In some cases a political unit can profit at the expense of others, but this is rarely possible and still more rarely achieved by the policies adopted, and is always to the disadvantage of the world as a whole.

5. ARTIFICIAL SPECIALIZATION OF MATERIAL AGENTS. DIVISION OF OPERATIONS LEADS TO INVENTION AND USE OF MACHINERY. Even natural resources are never used in their natural state. The process of developing and adapting them to particular uses is generally more or less of a specializing process and may be compared to the "education" of a human being. When we turn to the forms of productive equipment usually classed as artificial—tools, machines, buildings and the like, it is evident that specialization goes very far indeed. A tool or machine is usually much more specialized than a human being can ever be, and its efficiency in a particular task is connected with the degree of its specialization. Many things can be done, after a fashion, with a hammer; only one with an automatic printing-press or a watch-screw machine; but that one thing is done with wonderful precision and speed. Perhaps the very largest single source of gain from the specialization of labor is that it makes possible the development and use of machinery, the effectiveness of which is almost entirely a matter of its specialization to limited and relatively simple operations.

6. MINOR TECHNICAL GAINS. The gains from natural and artificial adaptation of men and things to tasks, plus that due to changing pieces of work instead of tasks (our No. 3 above) do not exhaust the economies of specialization. There is an economy in coordination due to the fact that a specialized worker need have access only to the

tools used for the operations he continuously performs, and not to all those used in making the article. This is practically rather an incidental matter, subordinate to the specialization of equipment. In primitive industry little is invested in tools, and a large investment carries with it specialization of both workers and equipment. We may note also as a final consideration in connection with this whole subject, that in many cases any sort of effective work involves the performance of different operations simultaneously, which of course necessitates specialization.

SOCIAL COSTS OF SPECIALIZATION. All the gains from specialization are summed up in the one word, *efficiency;* it enables us to get more goods, or better; its advantages are *instrumental.* On the other hand, specialization in itself, is an evil, measured by generally accepted human ideals. It gives us more products, but in its effects on human beings as such it is certainly bad in some respects and in others questionable. In the nature of the case [5] it means a narrowing of the personality; we like to see people of all-around, well-developed powers and capacities. In extreme instances, such as the monotonous work of machine-tending, or repetitive movements at a machine-forced pace, it may be ruinous to health and maddening to the spirit. In this connection it is especially significant that the most important source of gain also involves the most important human cost. The specialization of leadership means that the masses of the people work under conditions which tend to suppress initiative and independence, to develop servility as well as narrowness and in general to dehumanize them.

TECHNICAL COSTS OF ORGANIZATION. We have already mentioned the fact that there is another side to the technical advantages of specialization, namely the costs of as-

[5] Statements of this kind need a good deal of interpretation. In reality everything depends on the alternative system used as a basis of comparison. The idyllic system of universal craftsmanship certainly never existed historically; perhaps it could not exist; but we think we can imagine its existence.

sembly and distribution. This aspect of the situation is hinted at in the famous saying of Adam Smith that the division of labor is limited by the extent of the market, that is, really, by distribution costs. To these we must add the broader category of costs of organization in general. The existing social organization is called an "automatic" system, and in some respects it is such. But any system of bringing large numbers of people into intercommunication and coordinating their activities must involve enormous costs in actual human and physical energy. Organizations are like water-drops, or snow-balls or stones, or any large mass; the larger they are the more easily they are broken into pieces, the larger *in proportion* is the amount of energy that must be consumed in merely holding them together. The larger the army the bigger the proportion of officers, and the more unwieldy the aggregate, even then. The losses from this source in the modern world are stupendous; the number of persons, and still more the amount of brain power, which must be entirely taken up with passing on directions and keeping track of what is being done and "oiling the machinery" in one way and another is truly appalling. And the opportunity for persons to secure private gain by dislocating the organization machinery leads to still greater waste and loss.

INTERDEPENDENCE. A final important disadvantage of organized production and distribution is the resulting interdependence of persons and groups. This interdependence is supposed to be mutual, in the long run; but for the time being, the persons who perform such functions as coal mining and transportation are very much more necessary to, say, schools teachers or farmers than the latter are to them. Strikes or failures to function due to accidental causes produce a kind of suffering unknown in unorganized society, or even in small groups within which the pressure of public opinion is much more powerful. A phase of this interdependence manifests itself acutely in the ebb and flow of prosperity, particularly the recurrence of business crises bringing widespread distress.

Social Economic Organization

SOCIAL ORGANIZATION AND BIOLOGICAL ORGANISM: ANALOGY AND CONTRAST. As an introduction to the survey and classification of forms of social organization it will be useful to revert briefly to the comparison between economic society and the human body—especially to emphasize the fundamental difference. In this comparison the human individual is said to correspond to the "cell", the ultimate unit of biological structure. Individuals, like the cells in an animal body, are aggregated into "tissues" and "organs", which carry on the elementary life functions, seizing nourishment, transforming it into a condition suitable for use or digestion, distribution, disposal of waste, etc. The analogy is indeed obvious, and no doubt useful within limits, if it is kept on the level of analogy and not pressed too far. However, reasoning from analogy is always dangerous, and the conception of the "social organism" has probably produced more confusion than enlightenment. The differences between society and an animal organism are practically more important than the similarities, for it is in connection with the differences that the social problems arise.

The division of labor between the organs of the body is based on an innate differentiation of physical structure, and the coordination of their activities is automatic and mechanical. The cells or tissues do not choose what positions they will take up or what functions they will perform, nor can they change from one position or function to another. They do not meet with any of the problems which make the study of human organization a practical concern; they have no separate interests which may conflict with each other or with those of the body as a whole, and there can be no competition among them in any but a figurative sense.

Human society is the opposite of all this. Definite machinery has to be deliberately designed to reconcile or compromise between the conflicting interests of its members, who are separate purposive units; the organization

23

as a whole has no value in itself or purpose of its own, according to the dominant theory of democracy at least, but exists solely to promote the interests of its members. In the same way, as we have seen, planned provision must be made in human society for working out the division of labor, assigning the separate tasks to the various persons and apportioning productive equipment among them, for distributing the fruits of the activity, and even for determining the character of its own future life and growth.[6]

TYPES OF ORGANIZATION: 1. "STATUS" AND TRADITION, OR THE CASTE SYSTEM. The nearest approach to a mechanical division and coordination of activity which is reached or can be conceived of in human society would be a universal system of *status* or "caste". It is possible to imagine a social order in which elaborate specialization of activities is achieved on a purely customary basis, and some approximation to such an ideal is found in the caste system of India. We can suppose that rigid social custom might fix all the details of the division of occupations and technique of production, the assignment of individuals to their tasks being determined by birth, while tradition would also set the details of the standard of living for everyone. Such a society would have to be nearly unprogressive, though slow change in accordance with unconscious historical forces is compatible with the hypothesis.

There are two reasons for ascribing considerable theoretical importance to caste as a system of organization. It serves to bring out by contrast the characteristics of the modern Western system based on property and competition, a contrast made famous by Sir Henry Maine's theory that the transition from a régime of status to one of contract is a fundamental historical law. In the second place there is a large element of status in the freest society; social position, character of work and standard of living are determined even in America today, perhaps nearly as much by the "accident" of birth as by conscious or un-

[6] See also the discussion of insect societies (above p. 16) to which the observations made in regard to the animal organism will largely apply though in a lesser degree.

conscious selection in accord with innate personal traits. Moreover, any society based on the natural family as a unit tends toward progressively greater rigidity of stratification. With the passing of the frontier and the special conditions of a new country, rapid change in this direction has come to be a conspicuous feature of American life, though political and social motives have led us to set up opposing forces such as free education.

2. THE AUTOCRATIC OR MILITARISTIC SYSTEM. The first step away from a caste system in the direction of increasing freedom is represented by a centralized, autocratic system most briefly described by comparing it with the organization of an army. In such a social order, worked out to logical completeness, the whole structure of society, the division of labor, determination of policies, and allocation of burdens and benefits, would be dictated by an absolute monarch. The individual need not be asked what he wants or thinks good for him in the way of either his consumption or his share in production. The idea of organization itself might be worked out to any degree of intricacy, and coordination might indeed be highly effective. In practice, such a system would have to contain a large element of caste, unless the family were abolished entirely, as in Plato's scheme for an ideal republic. The organizing principle in an autocratic system is personal authority resting upon "divine", or prescriptive, right.

It is to be observed that this principle, while theoretically reduced to a minimum in modern society, is actually, like that of tradition and caste, very much in evidence. The exercise of "authority", while limited in degree, is as real as either "free" exchange or persuasion, within the family, in the internal organization of business units and in the "democratic" system of government itself. In an autocratic system worked out to ideal perfection, the population as well as all material goods would be the *property* of the monarch; the political and economic systems, as we habitually understand the terms today, would be completely fused, the ideas of sovereignty and property identified. A picture of such a social order may be found in the story of Joseph in Egypt, in the book of Genesis, after first the chattels of the people and then their persons were turned over to Pharaoh in exchange for the grain stored up by Joseph against the lean years. The theory of medieval European feudalism may be regarded as a combination of the principles of caste and of autocracy. This means that under feudalism also, there is no separation between the economic and political aspects of the social organization. The contrast in meaning between the two in the modern world will presently be looked into.

3. ANARCHISM AS A POSSIBLE SYSTEM. In the third type of organization mechanism to be considered, we swing to the extreme opposite of the two preceding, from rigorous control by tradition or arbitrary authority to absolute freedom, or purely voluntary association. Whether such a system is possible, may well be doubted, as most of the world does doubt; but it is at least conceivable, and many cultivated and noble minds have, as is well known, advocated attempting it as a practical program. The idea is simple enough; it is contended that if inequality and all hope or thought of exploiting or exercising authority over other men were abolished, people might agree voluntarily as to what were best to be done in the various contingencies of social life and the best method for doing it, and proceed accordingly, without any giving or taking of orders, or any threat of compulsion or restraint by force. It is not necessary to suppose that everyone would have to be all-knowing in regard to every sort of question. It is fully consistent with the theory of anarchy to have recourse to expert opinion; it must be assumed only that the experts would be able to agree, or that the mass of people would agree on which expert to recognize and follow. The theorists of philosophic anarchism who have attracted serious attention assign a large rôle to custom and the force of social opinion. There is no doubt that custom has in fact played the leading part in both originating and enforcing laws, especially in early times. But the case for anarchism in the sense of voluntary agreement through rational deliberation—that is, for this

system as opposed to a caste and custom organization—
is much less plausible. Apparently insuperable difficulties
stand in the way of the elimination of compulsion in an
intricate machine civilization subject to the stresses of
rapid material progress.

4. DEMOCRACY OR DEMOCRATIC SOCIALISM. The two systems remaining to be considered represent combinations
of or compromises between systems already named. The
first, democratic socialism, is a compromise between the
authoritarian and the anarchistic. The nearest approach
to the freedom of anarchy which we even theoretically
reach on any extended scale is the rule of the majority.
In its main structural features a society organized entirely
on this principle would resemble the autocratic, authoritarian system. The difference is that the controlling authority, instead of being an absolute autocrat, would itself be under the control of "public opinion", that is, the
will of the majority of the citizens, expressed through
some "political" apparatus. Again, the economic and political organizations would be fused and identified. This
is the type of social structure advocated in the main by
persons calling themselves "socialists" though by no
means to the exclusion of other types of organization
machinery, especially that of free bargaining. Custom
could not of course be excluded in any case, and competitive characteristics would undoubtedly appear, since
few socialists would absolutely prohibit market dealings.
The exercise of personal authority—beyond that involved
in the majority taking precedence over the minority in
cases of disagreement as to policy—would be reduced to
the minimum. It is hardly necessary to mention the fact
that the activities of modern societies are to a considerable and increasing extent organized "socialistically",
that an increasing fraction of their activities are carried
on under the mandatory direction of agencies selected by
majorities and as far as practicable made subject to the
will of the majority. Examples are the postal system, the
schools, streets and highways, the central banks and an
increasing proportion of public utility services.

The Economic Organization

5. THE EXCHANGE SYSTEM.   The last type of organization machinery to be distinguished is the one especially characteristic of modern Western nations, in which the whole system is worked out and controlled through exchange in an impersonal competitive market. It is variously referred to as the competitive system, the capitalistic system, the system of private property and free exchange, individual exchange cooperation, and so on. Its most interesting feature is that it is automatic and unconscious; no one plans or ever planned it out, no one assigns the participants their rôles or directs their functions. Each person in such a system seeks his own satisfaction without thought of the structure of society or its interests; and the mere mechanical interaction of such self-seeking units organizes them into an elaborate system and controls and coordinates their activities so that each is continuously supplied with the fruits of the labor of one vast and unknown multitude in return for performing some service for another multitude also large and unknown to him. Although the actuality diverges in many respects from such a simple idealized description, the results which are in fact achieved by this method are truly wonderful. Like the other systems described, it does not exist and can hardly be thought of as existing in a pure form. But so large a part of the ordinary work of the modern world is organized in this way that such expressions as "the present social system" or the "existing economic order", are commonly understood to refer to the organization of provision for the means of life through buying and selling.

TWO SUB-TYPES OF EXCHANGE ORGANIZATION: (A) HANDI-CRAFT, AND (B) FREE ENTERPRISE.   The first step in the description of the free exchange system must be to distinguish between two forms of it which differ in fundamental respects. That would be in the proper sense an exchange system or society, in which each individual produced a single commodity and exchanged his surplus of this, directly or through the medium of money, for the various other things required for his livelihood. Some approximation to this system existed in the handicraft organization of the medieval towns, and of course the farmers and a few city craftsmen of today typically produce concrete things to sell. We call this a "handicraft" system.

But such is by no means the characteristic form of modern economic organization. In modern industry in its most developed form no individual or small group can be said to "produce" anything. As it is sometimes put, we have gone beyond division of occupations to the division or subdivision of tasks. Typically, each individual merely performs some operative detail in the making of a commodity, or furnishes to some productive organization a part of the natural resources or capital it employs. But this difference in technology, as compared with a system where each person makes an entire article, is not so important as the difference in the personal relations, in the system of organization itself. In a handicraft system each one lives by producing and selling goods, and generally owns the material upon which he works and the article he makes when it is finished, as well as his shop or work place—most naturally in his home—and the tools or equipment used in performing his work.

In the modern free enterprise system, as exemplified in the large-scale industries, the relation of the individual to the system is of a quite different sort. As the worker produces nothing and owns nothing, he can exchange nothing, so far as want-satisfying goods are concerned. The individual in fact gets his living, not by selling and buying or exchanging *goods*, but by selling *productive services* for *money* and buying with the money the *goods* which he uses. And of course he does not carry out this exchange with other individuals, since they are in the same situation as himself, but typically with *business units*.

A business unit, or enterprise, is made up of individuals (among whom the man who sells to or buys from it may himself be included) but is distinct from these individuals and constitutes a fictitious person, company, a firm or typically a corporation. Production is now commonly carried on by such units. They are, of course, controlled by natural persons, but these "officers" act for the organization and not as individuals. Various separate persons (possibly with other business units as intermediaries) own and ultimately control any one business unit. The business unit itself partly owns but largely hires or leases from individuals (in some cases again indirectly) the productive power with which it operates, including the services of human beings and those of "property", natural and artificial.

It is a fact familiar to every reader of such a book as this that in the modern world economic activity has typically become organized in this form: *business units* buy productive services and sell products; *individuals or families* sell productive services and buy products. Hence the study of economics in our society is mainly the study of free enterprise.

The Price System and the Economic Process

MODERN ECONOMIC ORGANIZATION, AN "AUTOMATIC" SYS-TEM.   One of the most conspicuous features of organization through exchange and free enterprise, and one most often commented upon, is the absence of conscious design or control. It is a social order, and one of unfathomable complexity, yet constructed and operated without social planning or direction, through selfish individual thought and motivation alone. No one ever worked out a plan for such a system, or willed its existence; there is no plan of it anywhere, either on paper or in anybody's mind, and no one directs its operations.[1] Yet in a fairly tolerable way, "it works", and grows and changes. We have an amazingly elaborate division of labor, yet each person finds his own place in the scheme; we use a highly involved technology with minute specialization of industrial equipment, but this too is created, placed and directed by individuals, for individual ends, with little thought of larger social relations or any general social objective. Innumerable conflicts of interest are constantly resolved, and the bulk of the working population kept generally occupied, each person ministering to the wants of an unknown multitude and having his own wants satisfied by another multitude equally vast and unknown—

[1] This is true just insofar as the social order is in fact one of exchange and enterprise. We do have a large and increasing amount of deliberate planning and control in modern society, but this means precisely the substitution of "political" for "economic" methods of organization.

31

not perfectly indeed, but tolerable on the whole, and vastly better than each could satisfy his wants by working directly for himself. To explain the mechanism of this cooperation, unconscious and unintended, between persons whose feelings are often actually hostile to each other, is the problem of economic science. It is both a challenge to the intellectual interest, and of surpassing practical importance: for the workings of the system must be understood, if the action which society, in its self-conscious aspect is constantly taking in regard to it, is to result in good rather than harm.

PRICE, THE GUIDE AND REGULATOR. THE PRICE SYSTEM. The economic organization is built up and controlled, in a way familiar in its broad outlines to everyone, through the impersonal forces of *price*. The principles on which it operates are facts universally familiar; yet in their application to the practical problems of improving the working of the system, these principles not only become complicated, but run counter to natural and established ways of thinking. Many popular beliefs regarding economics and the effects of legislation are fallacies which when put into practice tend to impoverish the nation. On a general understanding of the fundamental laws of price relations, and on their thoughtful application in measures of public policy, rests all hope for prosperity under democratic institutions, all hope for efficiency in industry and a progressively more equitable distribution of the burdens and benefits of social cooperation in economic life.

The general theory of the system of free enterprise, as stated above, is simple. People get their "living" by selling productive power, meaning their own personal services or the use of property which they own, to industrial establishments, for money, and buying with the money the means of satisfying their wants and needs. They buy from industrial establishments also, generally from different ones than those to which they sell their own services, and generally through the medium of merchants or dealers. Industrial enterprises, reciprocally, buy productive services (of person and property) from individuals, use them to "produce" the means of want-satisfaction, and sell these to individuals. It is always to be kept in mind that our social organization is not simply and solely one of free enterprise. In agriculture particularly, in the professions largely, and in some other fields less extensively, we have production carried on on the "handicraft" principle; the family is the unit and uses its own productive power to make a product, which it sells in the market. Other productive operations are carried on by governmental agencies, which operate in various relations with the public and there are also some "cooperative" establishments. The typical modern business enterprise, however, is the corporation, an impersonal organization, which does buy or hire most of the productive power used in making the products which it sells. The process tends to be obscured by the fact that production of most things is divided into a great number of stages and branches, carried on in different establishments. Any single establishment commonly buys not only raw productive power, but various "products" of other establishments, together with some productive power, with which it turns out another "product", which in turn is probably not ready to satisfy wants, but is sold to still other establishments as "raw material". All these details will come in for discussion presently. In the meantime, it is possible to think of business establishments as a group, buying productive power from individuals, making products in the final sense, and selling these to individuals for "consumption" in satisfying their wants.

As explained in previous chapters, the general interest requires that the available productive power of society at large be used to create the means of satisfying the more important wants, as far as it will go, that it be used as efficiently as possible, that the total output of industry or social income be distributed equitably among the people, and that the productive equipment itself be maintained and reasonably improved. The general theory of free enterprise from this point of view—the provision made in such a system for realizing these objectives—can be stated briefly. Production is motivated and controlled by the consumers' expenditure of income. Each person being free to spend his money as he pleases, the presumption is that he will know the relative importance of his own various wants and will buy goods accordingly. Producers will then be compelled to furnish the things most in demand. They are placed in competition with each other; the establishment which conforms best to the wishes of consumers can sell its product at the highest prices, and one which does not produce things in demand may not be able to sell its wares at all. Whenever too much of anything is being made, in proportion to its importance to consumers, its price falls, and the price of things relatively short in supply rises. Producers therefore find it profitable to utilize productive power to make the things the public needs, or wants, in the correct proportions.

Moreover, producers are in competition in the purchase of productive power, and their means for purchasing are derived from the sale of products. Those who make products most in demand can pay higher prices for labor, materials, etc., and it is assumed that those who furnish these things will sell them to those who offer to pay most. Thus it is not a matter of choice with the producer. He is literally compelled to meet the consumers' demands as accurately as his competitiors do, or he cannot secure productive power, and cannot remain in business.

In the same way, the competition of producers tends to force them to be as *efficient* as possible in the conduct of their operations. For those who succeed in turning out the largest quantity of any commodity with the use of a given amount of productive power can pay most for it, and force less efficient competitors either to adopt more efficient methods or to go out of business. Thus every detail in the production process is constantly subjected to a ruthless process of selection in a struggle for existence, and an irresistible pressure is brought to bear toward the use of productive power both in the "best" direction and in accord with methods of the highest possible efficiency.

The payments made by producers for productive power, including labor and the use of capital and natural resources, constitute the incomes of individuals. Competition of producers, and the effort of each individual to secure as large an income as he can in exchange for the services he furnishes to production, *tend* to make these payments equal to the full value of every service in its most productive use. Thus the distribution of income is worked out on the principle of paying each individual in accord with his contribution to the total social product, as measured by the amount consumers are willing to pay. Consumers also compete with each other, those who will pay the most for any product get it, and this competition tends to assure to the individual who furnishes any produtive service a payment for its use equal to the value of the most valuable contribution which that service can be made to yield. The relation of the system to the fourth primary task of organization, that is, to maintenance and progress, can only be mentioned here. It is surely evident that rich rewards are waiting for those who can introduce improved methods of production, or bring new resources into use, while those who only patiently accumulate capital to make possible the increase and improvement of productive equipment in its commonest forms are rewarded with interest on savings.

PRINCIPLES VERSUS FACTS. EXPLANATION VERSUS JUSTIFICATION OR CRITICISM. Such is the enterprise system in a brief "airplane" view, and according to the accepted theories of economics, which are undoubtedly sound if not pushed beyond such an outline of fundamental tendencies. In such a view, the system appears both extremely simple and altogether beneficent. But when these few abstract principles are clothed with the concrete facts of life, which is the task of economic science, it quickly develops that economic relations are far from simple and the results achieved not only far from ideal in the sense of creating universal happiness but also far from what we have a reasonable right to expect. Our task of putting the complex and often unlovely flesh and viscera of reality upon this clean white skeleton of abstract principle must be carried out in several stages. Only a few of the earlier stages can be sketched in this volume, and we must be concerned primarily with the more general sources of error in understanding the way in which the system actually works. Discussion in detail of its failures and the problems involved in attempting to remedy them must be left to more extensive and specialized treatises. The factual basis of these failures and problems will, however, be indicated from time to time and given such emphasis as the scope of our study permits.

It must constantly be borne in mind that explaining how the system works does not mean justification of it, as it has a way of seeming to do. On the contrary, a clear understanding of the competitive mechanism will make obvious fundamental weaknesses in its very nature, and is chiefly important in this connection, through pointing the way to intelligent procedure looking to its improvement. Two or three of the main hidden assumptions which partly account for the confusion of explanation and justification may be mentioned here at the outset and these and others will be emphasized from time to time. In the first place, it is not true that producers and consumers will necessarily be in competition among themselves if left to pursue their own interests individually. Groups of either may, and often will, combine in one way or another to form *monopolies,* and much conscious social interference is called for to counteract this tendency. Again, it must be borne in mind that the controlling force considered above is *pecuniary demand,* which for many reasons does not constitute a valid measure of the real human importance of products. Demand depends upon the desire and the purchasing power of consumers. But desires may be manufactured by fraud or corruption of tastes, and at best it cannot be assumed that what people individually want is uniformly what is best for them or for society. Still less is want, as measured by purchasing power, a perfect index of real value. The vicious wants of a degenerate heir of millions or of a successful crook may outweigh in their pull upon productive power the requirements for a decent livelihood of hundreds of poor families.

In regard to the mere explanation of how the competitive system works, we may observe that the chief difficulties arise from the interconnections between different goods and the different satisfactions they afford, and between different means of production. It is hardly ever true that a single kind of want-satisfaction is derived exclusively from a single commodity. Interactions are of both the possible sorts—it may take a combination of goods to satisfy a single want, or the same want, or nearly the same, may be satisfied by various goods. On the one hand, automobiles are useless without gasoline, and on the other, bread may be made of various grains, or other starchy vegetables. The two relations may even go together; butter and bread enhance each other's usefulness, and yet as both are foods, either may more or less take the place of the other. With productive agencies, this combination of opposite relations is universal. Neither land nor labor nor capital alone can produce any wheat, yet within limits each may be substituted for the other in production.

SUBDIVISION OF THE PROBLEM. THE NOTION OF AN UNPRO-GRESSIVE SOCIETY OR "STATIC STATE". In setting out to explain the workings of the economic system, it is convenient to make a sharp separation between the first three of the four main functions of organization and the fourth function. Society is at any time using economic power for two sets of purposes—first, to satisfy current wants, and second, to provide for maintenance and progress. It will simplify our task of explanation very materially to consider these two processes separately. First, we shall take up the organization of existing resources for the satisfaction of existing wants and their use in accordance with an existing level of technological arts and sciences. Then the explanation will be expanded to take in the effects of activities directed toward increasing the stock of resources, changing the wants and improving the technology. That is, we shall first discuss the economic system as if it were concerned with the first problem alone, as it would be if no changes in resources, wants and technology were taking place.

Neglecting, provisionally, the effects of these progressive changes, will greatly simplify the problem, without falsifying it in essential respects. For the two aspects of economic life are in fact largely distinct. The organization for satisfying current wants has essentially the same character that it would have if the progressive changes were to cease—except only that a certain fraction of a nation's total productive energy is always being employed in these fields which minister to progress. The fraction, however, is not very large. It is not accurately known, but in the United States, expert estimates place it at about one-sixth. That is, about five-sixths of our productive power is actually used for producing goods and services for day-to-day consumption and about one-sixth for improvements of all sorts. This conception of an economic society where *all* the productive power is used for satisfying current wants, where no progress takes place, is in general use in economic discussion and is called a "static" society. It is true that activities promoting progress, besides drawing off their fraction of productive energy, disturb and modify the workings of the "static" organization in important respects. Yet is is useful to understand the tendencies of competitive relations as they would be in the absence of such disturbances, and the interference of progressive changes in the static adjustment can best be taken up in connection with the discussion of progress as a separate problem. The use of the "static hypothesis" is necessary, both to simplify the discussion, and because in practice the effects of progressive changes are not important in connection with a large proportion of business and social problems. With reference to other problems, involving adjustments looking a long distance into the future, this procedure would give rise to inaccuracy; and the effects of progressive changes have to be taken into account, as far as they can be foreseen. In addition, progress itself constitutes one of the major problems, or groups of problems, of social policy, and therefore of economic science.

THE ECONOMIC PROCESS IN A "STATIC" VIEW. Disregarding the progressive changes, economic society becomes a process of utilizing productive energy in the satisfaction of human wants, in accord with certain methods, which represent the existing state of material civilization. These three elements or sets of elements, namely (1) productive resources, (2) the wants and tastes of the population, and (3) the existing development of technical methodology, constitute the *data*, the given factors with which an economic system works. With reference to them, as they are at any given time, competitive forces are tending to establish a certain stable adjustment of the process of production, distribution and consumption. That is, the process of competitive buying and selling, tends to establish a condition in which certain means of production would be used to create certain want-satisfying goods and in which these goods would reach and be consumed by certain individuals, and that the flow of productive services into industries and of goods from industries to persons, would be a steady and unchanging process, because the forces acting upon each phase of the process would be in equilibrium.

This process of want-satisfaction falls into numerous stages, as well as branches ramifying through each other. The wants to be satisfied are numerous, and the goods which satisfy them even more so. Those things which satisfy wants directly are usually made, or "produced", by the use of other things, materials and agencies, these in turn by still others, and so on, in an indefinite and widely varying number of stages. The stages in the process of making the direct means of want-satisfaction give rise to indirect or intermediate goods, which also enter into exchange, are bought and sold. The series from direct to indirect and more and more indirect means or agencies must end somewhere, in things and agencies which are not the result of previous economic activity or productive operations.[2] These most indirect, or final, means of want-

[2] Practically speaking, the series must be treated as ending somewhere. Whether it really does end is more doubtful. The so-called "natural resources" also have a history. Just where the series practically ends at a given time, it is not easy to say. These questions will recur from time to time as the discussion progresses.

satisfaction sometimes operate directly, there being no intermediate stages, as when a piece of land is prized as a dwelling site or for its natural beauty, or when one person sings a song or cures a disease for another; or there may be a vast number of intermediate stages, as when iron ore (an unproduced agency) is used in making steel, which is used to make machines and these to make other machines, which make tools to make other machines and so on indefinitely, until perhaps we have a locomotive which hauls coal which is burned to warm a house. It is necessary to have terms by which to designate various stages and instrumentalities in the economic process. The everyday use of terms like goods, wealth, income, wants, resources, etc., is loose and often too ambiguous for the purposes of scientific discussion. Some space will now be devoted to a more detailed analysis of the process and to definition of certain terms necessary to distinguish the elements which have to be distinguished with a degree of accuracy.

THE ELEMENTARY CONCEPTS OF ECONOMICS.   From the point of view just suggested, the economic process is a succession of operations using means to achieve ends. The ultimate end is the satisfaction of wants. The direct means of want-satisfaction are consumption goods, such as food, clothing, houses, books, motor-cars, etc., and personal services, such as medical attention, the ministrations of musicians, actors, preachers, barbers, domestics, etc., which satisfy wants in other ways than by providing consumable material goods. Intermediate goods comprise the material productive equipment of industry, the factories, stores, and other buildings, railroads, mines, and everything but man himself and the ultimate materials and forces of nature. These in turn—man and nature—together with an element in the intermediate goods which we call "capital" and whose nature will have to be explained—constitute ultimate resources.

The whole series may be roughly represented by a diagram, in connection with which the elements will be further and more carefully considered.

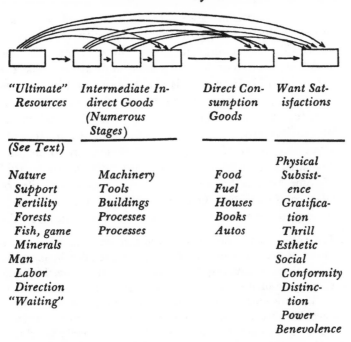

"Ultimate" Resources	Intermediate In- direct Goods (Numerous Stages)	Direct Con- sumption Goods	Want Sat- isfactions
(See Text)			
			Physical
Nature	Machinery	Food	Subsist-
Support	Tools	Fuel	ence
Fertility	Buildings	Houses	Gratifica-
Forests	Processes	Books	tion
Fish, game	Processes	Autos	Thrill
Minerals			Esthetic
Man			Social
Labor			Conformity
Direction			Distinc-
"Waiting"			tion
			Power
			Benevolence

In this scheme the squares may be thought of as representing the materials which pass from one stage to the next. The long arrows indicate that any or all of the intermediate stages may be skipped. It is especially important to note two things: First, the services of man and nature are combined with materials at each stage in carrying forward to the next stage the sequence of indirect goods. Second, both nature and man, as already observed, may satisfy wants directly. Nature affords standing room and esthetic gratification (including the emotions of wonder and awe, as well as love of beauty) and a human being may render service directly in innumerable ways (including again the service of exhibiting himself as a "wonder" of one sort or another—dramatics, professional sports, etc.). In connection with the several stages of the economic process, or combinations of them, are a number of concepts which call for definition or brief explanation.

WANTS AND THE DIRECT MEANS OF SATISFYING WANTS. At the end of the economic process is the satisfaction of human wants, and wants afford the motive power which actuates the entire process.[3] The main types of wants are indicated by headings in connection with the diagram above. The most important fact about wants, and one which we have to notice in various connections is that the behavior of civilized man is chiefly explained by motives distinctly above, though connected with, the biological urge to maintain and propagate physical life. Food, clothing, shelter, etc., are called subsistence wants, but it is obvious that most of the effort we expend in connection with them is directed toward conformity to "standards" of some kind rather than maintenance of actual life, or even comfort. These facts introduce deceptive complications into the relation between the commodities and the

[3] Attention should be called to the fact that two relations between wants and economic activity are included in the statement given. Wants may be thought of as the "objective" end, or purpose of the process, or as the cause or "explanation" of it. There is an important opposition, and not merely a difference, between the two conceptions. From the one viewpoint, want-satisfaction is the end which the process *ought* to achieve, and the problem of economics is chiefly that of explaining why it falls short of complete accomplishment of its purpose. From the other viewpoint, which regards wants as the cause of activity, it is axiomatic that wants are really satisfied. There is in fact a fundamental conflict between these two viewpoints, which runs through all our thinking about human behavior. Such problems, and others related to them, raise philosophical questions as to the interpretation of human life and its relation to natural processes which have to be left to the philosophical specialist. For the purposes of scientific discussion, we have to adopt the second point of view, treating want-satisfaction as cause rather than as end or objective. The task of the scientist is the *explanation* of what happens, by formulation of causal laws. It is always necessary, however, to recognize that the practical point of view reverses the theoretical. Economics has no practical significance unless it is possible for man to control his behavior, in a real sense, by taking thought about it, which implies that it is not altogether mechanically determined by external causes.

From a third point of view, advocated by many modern psychologists, as they call themselves, wants are entirely metaphysical and unreal and the only reality is the way in which an individual "behaves" in a given situation.

wants they satisfy. Though it may seem paradoxical, the evident truth is that the most divergent commodities may be used to satisfy essentially the same wants; the same kind of satisfaction which one consumer gets from a luxuriously appointed table another may secure through elegant dress, another through motor cars and still another, perhaps, from a strong-box well filled with "gilt-edged" securities.

CONSUMPTION; GOODS AND SERVICES; UTILITY, THE LAW OF DIMINISHING UTILITY. Want-satisfaction is, in its economic aspect, called "consumption". Not all want-satisfaction is of economic interest, but only that which involves effort and thought or use of means of some sort, and involves in addition, some relation to other human beings in society. The means of want-satisfaction are *goods* or the *services* of goods, and the *services of persons*. The property possessed by goods or services of being able to satisfy wants is *utility*.[4] Those goods which do not call for thought or effort, and are outside the field of economic discussion, are commonly called *free goods*, in contrast with *economic goods*. Examples of free goods are air and sunshine, and, under natural conditions, water. Free goods are distinguished by the fact that they exist in super-abundance, or cannot be controlled or appropriated (sunshine), while economic goods are those which are appropriable and limited in supply in relation to the need or desire for them.

In relation to economic life, the most important fact about the want for any particular commodity is its satiability. The more one has of any single good the less important it becomes to get an additional unit, or to keep

[4] Again it is appropriate to utter a warning in regard to the dual meaning of wants. From the strictly scientific point of view, utility, as the cause of action, is the power to arouse desire rather than that of affording satisfaction. It is evident that the two are by no means the same thing; yet it is practically necessary to treat them as identical, leaving refinements in distinctions to the philosopher, as suggested above. From the "behavioristic" point of view, again, action is caused by the situation, and the notion of a want is superfluous.

any one unit in the supply already possessed. This principle is called the *law of diminishing utility*. It explains the diversification of consumption, if not the precise amounts of every commodity purchased by any individual. In the absence of this fact of human nature, a person would spend his entire income on some one commodity, the first one on which he happened to get started, or the one considered most important to begin with. In consequence of the principle of diminishing utility, expenditure for any commodity is stopped at the point where some other commodity offers a more attractive use for income. Economic utility does not mean the usefulness of a thing in the abstract, but the importance of any one unit of the available supply. This accounts for the old paradox that while coal is so much more useful to the human race than diamonds it is worth so much less by the ton. When a thing is superabundant, like the air, it clearly has no economic utility at all, though it may be indispensable to life.

INCOME, UTILITY, VALUE AND PRICE.   Strictly speaking, all consumption is consumption of services. The relation between the different types of goods and the services they render will be discussed presently. The aggregate of consumption or of services consumed, in a unit of time, by a person or a group, may be called *income*. In determining income, each type of commodity consumed (or satisfaction enjoyed) is measured by the economic utility of that type of commodity, in view of the amount of it actually consumed and the purchasing power of the consumers. Since the economic utility of a unit of any commodity decreases as the number of units consumed increases, the total economic utility of a large consumption of wheat, say, or sugar, may be smaller than it would be if the total consumption were smaller and the satisfaction accompanying it more intense. This principle is often manifested in terms of money price in the fact that a large crop of wheat or cotton may bring less in the aggregate than a small crop, the price per unit being lower in greater ratio than the crop is larger. The principle is referred to in economic literature as the "paradox" of utility or of ex-

44

change value. In determining the income of a group, by adding the incomes of the individuals composing it, we have to assume that the utility of the same unit of the same commodity (the amount of income it represents) is the same for every person into whose consumption that commodity enters. In this respect, also, economic utility diverges strikingly from the common-sense idea of the real value or importance of things. From the common-sense point of view it is absurd to think of a loaf of bread as representing the same amount of satisfaction to a dyspeptic rich man as it does to a hungry laborer. But the price *is the same* to both, and that is the fact which is decisive from the standpoint of economic science.[5]

The term *value* is used in different senses in economic literature. Like the term utility, it is sometimes an ethical quantity, the "real" value of a thing, in contrast with its money value under some set of conditions, and sometimes it is simply the money value or price. In this book value will be used exclusively to denote exchange value or

[5] Again, the reader may be reminded that there is a wide contrast between the point of view of a scientific explanation of facts and that of the human interpretation or evaluation of the same facts. Money incomes do not correctly measure human values. Another reservation in regard to income is in order. It is defined above as the *consumption* of an individual or group, in a unit of time (ordinarily a year). In the unprogressive or static society, the production and consumption of any year would be equal, and income might be defined with reference to either indifferently. In reality, this is not so; as already remarked, an appreciable fraction of the productive effort of any year appears as improvement of various sorts, new wealth or other provision for an increased flow of consumption in the future. Although economists generally consider that logically, income ought to be defined as the consumption during a given interval, statistical practice and accounting methods and our habitual ways of thinking view it rather as the *production*. The increase in wealth of an individual or nation is generally considered as part of its income for the year, in addition to what he consumes. This really involves double counting, since wealth is valued only for its product, and the product of the wealth accumulated in a given year is counted in the income of succeeding years.

money value practically speaking as measured by price. Price and value will be distinguished, if at all, only in the case where some temporary and accidental circumstance causes goods to be sold at a price notably different from that which would be established by the ordinary working of economic tendencies. In regard to the word utility, no effort will be made to stick to a uniform usage, but care will be taken to make the context show clearly which of its various meanings is intended. In general, it should also be restricted in scientific economic discussion to designation of the actual cause of value, or of the choices which determine value and price; if this is done, utility also is equal to value, and an aspect of value. Value is expressed in terms of money, and money price is the practical measure of economic services. The relation between utility and price will come up again in the next lesson.

GOODS AND THEIR SERVICES. CAPITALIZATION AND WEALTH. Economically significant services, direct and in various degrees indirect, are rendered by persons or by things. Most of the power to render salable services, possessed by either a person or a thing, is the result of the previous expenditure upon or investment in the person or thing of other services of persons and things, and the notion of "ultimate" resources calls for much interpretation. The productive power of society, in both the material and the personal forms, is kept up from year to year and from generation to generation by the expenditure of productive power—in rearing and training new human beings to replace those who die or pass the age of usefulness, and in producing new material instrumentalities (including the rearing and training of animals and cultivation of plants) to replace those which wear out. In addition, modern Western nations are making some increase, in normal years, both in their human population and their material equipment. It is not inaccurate to say that the entire productive capacity of any modern nation has been built up in this cumulative process; the value of the productive power invested in human and material equipment in the course of history would probably be equal to the total "capitalized" value of that productive power at the present time.

Many of the problems of wealth and production center in this word "capitalization". We may begin with the statement, to which there are no exceptions, that *wealth is capitalized income* or service. The term wealth or property is used to designate all exchangeable things or goods, whether they derive their value from the power to satisfy wants directly or from that of serving indirectly in the making of other goods which serve less indirectly or directly. Capitalization is the process by which the value of a service or time-stream of service to be rendered by a good in the future becomes reflected in the present exchange value of the good itself. If the service-yielding good is indestructible and the value of its service for any one year is known and assumed to be unchanging through the future, capitalization consists in the simple operation of finding the sum of money which if put at interest at the current rate [6] would yield an income equal to the annual value of the service in question. Thus if a piece of land can be leased to bring in a rental of a thousand dollars per year, and the going rate of interest is five per cent, the land will be worth one thousand dollars divided by five-hundredths, or twenty thousand dollars. If the income is not permanent or is expected to change in value in the future, the operation is less simple but the capitalized value can be found for any given conditions by a little algebra or by the use of formulas or tables published for the purpose.

The second observation is that *the earnings of human beings cannot be capitalized,* for the simple reason that the laws of modern nations do not permit human beings to be bought and sold, by other human beings or by themselves; consequently, they *are not wealth.* One can buy the service of a material thing a day at a time or a year at a time, or buy the thing itself outright, which means to buy at once all the services it will ever render, as long as it may endure. But with human beings one can

[6] The meaning of interest will receive brief attention in a later section of this lesson and the explanation of the rate of interest will be given in the chapter on "Distribution".

only buy their services as they are rendered; one cannot buy a human being as such, nor in general buy his services for any appreciable time in the future by making a labor contract. Such contracts are now generally unenforceable, particularly in the United States, and can rarely, and exceptionally, be bought and sold. Hence, while wealth is capitalized income, there is much income which is not capitalized into wealth; in the United States the fraction is about three-fourths of the total for the nation; this amount represents services rendered by human beings, only about one-fourth of our national income being the services of salable goods or wealth.

This distinction between human beings and wealth rests on institutional facts, but is fundamental to the interpretation of modern economic relations. In a slave society, it need hardly be said, matters would stand otherwise; human beings would be wealth, as horses and cattle are now, and the distinction between labor and wealth services would fall away, as far as the enslaved part of the population were concerned. Even in our present social order, human productive capacity may approach to a condition resembling in many respects that of an owned material agency. A young man may borrow money to procure for himself an education in medicine or engineering and use the earnings derived from his training to pay interest on its cost and repay the principal, just as he would do if he had bought a house and leased it for a rental. Yet the fact remains that he could sell the house, and he cannot sell his education, or separate the use of it from himself (nor sell himself outright). And because the education or other human capacity cannot be sold, no definite price can be fixed as the measure of its value. Moreover, the value, as accurately as it can be ascertained, will not show a tendency to equal its cost or the investment incurred in producing it, to anything like the same degree as will be true of the value and cost of houses and other freely producible income-yielding wealth.

There may seem to be wealth which does not inhere in material things, but examination will reveal that this generally is not so. A mortgage, for instance, represents a division in the ownership of the mortgaged chattel, or the income yielded by it. Even a patent-right or the good-will of a highly advertised product represents conditions attaching to the use of material productive equipment, making it yield an extra income as compared with similar agencies in other uses. Exceptions are indeed possible; an unsecured promissory note given by a man who has only his earning power may have a certain sale value in a community where the man is known for competence and integrity. The value of such a note may be regarded as the capitalization of a small and indefinite portion of the man's earning-power over a limited interval in the future.[7]

PRODUCTION: THE CREATION OF SALABLE VALUE OR UTILITY. Production is defined in economics to include both (a) the rendering of salable direct services, that is, satisfaction of wants, and (b) the imparting of sale value, or increased sale value, to goods, whether direct or indirect. This usage is somewhat different from that of the business world, which would hardly include the first at all, and not all of the second. The business man distinguishes production from distribution in a different way than does economics. In the scientific literature, that is, storage, transportation, finance and selling are treated as part of the production process, because they also, directly or in-

[7] There are many problems in connection with measuring the wealth and income of a nation which space limits preclude our taking up here. For instance, if the homework of wives alone were to be valued at ordinary servants' wages, the estimates of the national income of the United States would be increased from one-fourth to one-third. In general, statistics of income include only those services which are either actually exchanged for money or are of kinds usually exchanged for money. Other services which persons perform for themselves or for their own families without pay are left out. It must always be remembered too that an increase in the money value of any item may represent increased valuation due to scarcity, and may indicate less want-satisfaction than before. This is likely to be true of rent on land and natural resources. It goes without saying that all income and wealth comparisons must be corrected for differences in the value of the dollar or other unit of value in which they may be stated.

directly, create want-satisfying power, just as truly as the operations of agriculture or manufacturing. This view is commonly emphasized by a classification of the "utilities" or kinds of direct want-satisfying power which a good may possess and which are imparted to it in the production process. These include the utilities of *form, space, time, and possession.* It is evident without elaboration that a thing has greater power to satisfy wants where it is more wanted than where it is less wanted, and that consequently transportation is a productive operation; also that want-satisfying power may be increased by preserving a good from a time of no need or of abundance to a time of greater need or scarcity, as when ice is stored in winter or food products in summer; likewise in the case of transferring a good from a person whose want (as measured by willingness and ability to pay) is less to one whose want is greater. This analysis of utility is designed to correct the popular fallacy that merchandising, storage, finance, etc., are unproductive or of no value socially in contrast with the industries which create "form" utility. In fact, the former industries render a service indispensable to the consumer, and commonly render it much more cheaply than he could possibly do for himself. If it is practicable to perform any of these functions more economically than it is now done, anyone who can demonstrate the fact can make his fortune in short order.

Production also includes the rendering of "personal services", as already discussed, and the direct utilization of want-satisfying powers and qualities in nature, as well as the processing of intermediate goods and storing up of utility in them. It does *not* include the rearing and training of human beings, for the reason that persons and their productive capacities are not salable, and have no definite value, though as already pointed out the aim and import of these activities may be similar in many fundamental respects to the creation of property value.

TYPES OF GOODS. PERISHABLE AND DURABLE, DIRECT AND INDIRECT GOODS OR ATTRIBUTES OR USES OF GOODS.   The relations which an article, that is service-yielding and scarce, and hence economically significant, and hence valuable, sustains to economic problems, depend largely on two distinctions. The first is the *direct* or *indirect* nature of the service it renders, whether it satisfies wants or is instrumental in the production of something which satisfies them. A second division intimately connected with this and cutting across it separates goods into *perishable* and *durable*. Some goods render service only once, being destroyed in consumption, like food and fuel. Others render a succession or stream of services, such as a piece of furniture, a machine or a farm. There are of course all degrees of durability, ranging from the absolute perishability [8] of food and fuel, through tools and equipment of longer and longer life to the absolute permanence (for human purposes) of geographical features, statues, etc. There are also all degrees of directness and indirectness; and since practically any degree of durability may go with any degree of directness or indirectness, an exhaustive classification of goods from the two standpoints together is out of the question. The same article, too, may have both direct and indirect uses, as coal may be burned to heat houses or to furnish power for production, wheat may be human food or stock-feed, etc. Moreover, "extremes meet"; as already observed, an ultimate resource may render service directly, as nature furnishes standing room and support and scenic beauty. Natural goods which are both unproduced and direct may have all degrees of durability.

For illustration, a classification giving examples of the extremes of both scales, of durability and directness, and one intermediate degree of each, is given in the following table. It is to be remarked that the fertility of the soil, one

[8] It will be noted that perishability and durability are defined for economic purposes with reference to use. Coal, or even some foods, may last indefinitely if not used, but economically are perishable goods because they cannot be used without being completely destroyed. On the other hand, the physical permanence of many useful things, including objects of beauty, is quite independent of use or non-use. This is true of sunsets, wild flowers, the beauty of autumn woods, and the freshness and charm of spring, also of the productive potency of each season after its own fashion.

	Direct goods	Indirect (produced for use in further production)	"Ultimately Unproduced" (See Text)
Perishable (Destroyed in one act of use)	(Also wild fruit, nuts, etc.) Fuel (in houses) (Natural or prepared)	Feed for stock	(Also wild fruit, nuts, etc., both direct and un-produced)
Semi-durable	Clothing, furniture, pleasure cars, also wild flowers	Lumber, tools, machines, buildings,— capital goods typically	Natural abrasives. An unimproved road (also wild flowers)
Completely durable	Natural scenery, climate (also many art works) (Also permanent landscaping)	Drainage works, tunnels, dams & other permanent improvements on land, for productive purposes. Building stone and brick.	Ocean and natural waterways (also natural scenery, both direct and un-produced)

of the most important forms of wealth, is not found in the table. It can hardly be classified and might in fact fall in any compartment of either the second or the third column. That is, it may be either natural or produced and may have any degree of permanence, depending on the way in which it is used; it could not fall in the first column, as its usefulness is always more or less indirect. Another fact of interest is that the significance of a good directly useful in the physical sense is not uncommonly indirect to the individual owner, who leases it to others to secure a money income. In regard to durability, we have remarked above that the useful life of a thing may stand in various relations to the physical permanence of the qualities which give it value. Some things, like coal, have indefinite permanence when not used, but an absolutely limited capacity for service; others, like a cut flower, have a limited life quite independent of whether they are enjoyed or not; still others may last longer under reasonable use than in disuse, as is said to be the case with electric storage batteries. Of especial importance is the fact that the *use* or *service* itself of a good whose life is independent of the service it renders is absolutely *perishable*. This includes all indestructible goods as well as those of limited life, and is also in large part true of human beings; the hour's use, product or enjoyment, is irrecoverably gone when the hour is past.

PRODUCTIVE CONSUMPTION. Of the whole production process, viewed on a national or world scale, the greater part consists of using indirect goods and services to convert materials into less and less indirect forms, to carry them forward toward the condition in which they will satisfy some human want. Actual rendering of want-satisfying service is certainly the smaller part of the total. In this last stage of the process, production and consumption merge, the rendering and the utilization or enjoyment of the service taking place in the same act. In the indirect portion of production, more-indirect goods and services of course disappear, and are naturally said to be consumed; coal, wheat, labor, etc., are "consumed" in making bread. In a deeper sense, however, the coal and wheat are not consumed or destroyed. Rather their utilities are converted into other forms and carried forward into the bread itself, to be consumed when this is eaten. This relation is often emphasized by designating the utilization of intermediate goods and services in the making of more direct goods as *productive consumption*. The notion is important especially in connection with the valuation of the goods which result. With a qualification regarding time (see below), the value of any product, intermediate or final, is the cumulative sum of the values of all the ultimate services which have become embodied in it through previous stages of the production process, and the value of any productive service is the anticipated value of the consumption service it will ultimately render.

The Economic Organization

PRODUCERS' AND CONSUMERS' GOODS AND WEALTH. Logically speaking, the expression, producers' goods or wealth, coincides with indirect utility and consumers' goods with direct. In strict logic, all *goods* are *indirect;* only *services* are consumed, and all goods are significant through yielding or producing services. In practice, however, it is not feasible to adhere to rigid classifications. The production process is conveniently regarded as ending when the product reaches the hands of the final consumer. Such further productive operations as holding a good until its service is wanted, cooking and serving food, and the like, are ignored.[9] In this connection, again, the same piece of property, such as a house, might be regarded as a productive good if leased to another person and as a consumption good if used by another, the owner. A good cannot be leased unless it has a considerable measure of durability (think of leasing meat or coal!) and for this and other reasons there is a tendency to restrict the notion of producers' wealth to things which are both indirect and durable—though coal for use in a factory, locomotive or steamship would certainly be placed in this class.

THE MEASUREMENT OR VALUATION OF GOODS AND OF SERVICES. THE RÔLE OF TIME IN PRODUCTION AND CONSUMPTION. CAPITALIZATION, CAPITAL GOODS AND CAPITAL. A rather careful analysis of the production process, particularly of the rôle of intermediate goods, is required to avoid confusion as to the nature of productive power and the conditions of its economical employment—the essence of economic policy. The basic principle is that productive power never has any value in itself, but is significant only for the want-satisfying service which it ultimately represents

[9] As already pointed out, the usage of economists is much more logical than that of business men and everyday non-scientific discussion. In the latter, production is regarded as ending with the last physical transformations the product undergoes, the rest of what economists include in production, storage, transportation, merchandising, etc., being called distribution. In economics, "distribution" has another meaning, being used to designate the process by which the total income of society is divided or distributed among individuals.

and is measured in every case by the amount of that service or utility, for consumption. The general theory of valuation, explaining how the prices of direct and indirect goods and services of persons and of goods are determined and how different prices are interrelated, belongs to later stages of the discussion, but one elementary fact calls for emphasis here. It is that unless time or waiting is counted as a productive service, the value of a good is not necessarily equal either to the total value of the service it renders during its useful life nor to the total value of the services actually expended upon and embodied in it in the course of its production. Value is ultimately service value only; but the quantity of value depends not only on the quantity of the service, unless time is counted as a service, but also on *the way in which a given quantity is distributed in time.* Time affects both consumption and production. An apple-tree which would yield a hundred bushels of apples in one year would be worth very much more than one which yielded a bushel a year for a hundred years, which is simply to say that a hundred units of a given commodity in hand now are worth more than the certainty of receiving a hundred units spread over a long interval of time. From the production side, similarly, a structure whose erection called for the labor of a hundred men for a hundred years would represent much more value when it was finished than one which could be erected by ten thousand men in one year, all other conditions being the same, of course. That is, the same total quantity of physical productive effort, the same number of man-years of labor in this case, can produce more value when expended over a long period of time than when expended in a short period.

In short, *time itself has value.* And it has value for two reasons. First, it has value in connection with consumption, for the simple and obvious reason that men do not care to postpone all their enjoyment of goods and services into the indefinite future, but, beyond certain limits, prefer a smaller amount of consumption in the present to a greater amount in the future. They will not "wait", not indefinitely at least, without being paid for doing it. Second, time has value in connection with production. The final reason for this is the well-known fact that if one is in a position to wait a considerable time for a product, he can obtain more of it by the expenditure of the same total quantity of productive power, than if he has to have it immediately, because in the first case it is possible to construct tools, machines, etc., and prepare conditions which greatly increase the efficiency of productive effort. It is a general rule that the longer the series of intermediate products is permitted to be, the greater is the total product which can be obtained by the expenditure of the same total quantity or productive power—provided, of course, that the whole process is intelligently planned. That is, *time is a form of productive power.* Of course, time alone cannot produce commodities, but in that respect it is no different from other productive agencies, for neither can labor or natural resources produce except in cooperation with each other, and with time.

The significance of time appears, in the valuation of an indirect service, in the form of a *discounting* of the direct, consumption service it will finally render, in accordance with its distance in the future. If it were not for such a discount on futurity, the value of any permanent productive resource would evidently be infinite, as there is no limit to the quantity of service ultimately obtainable from it by waiting sufficiently long. The rate of discount is the rate of interest. The way in which the rate of interest is determined is a phase of the problem of distribution, to be discussed in a later chapter, where it will appear that the effect of using a longer time for production in increasing the efficiency of production is the dominant consideration. As production progresses, goods ripening toward readiness for use, interest appears as a "carrying charge" on the value of productive power already expended upon them. The accumulation of this carrying charge, or the decrease of the amount of discount to which their future services are subject as they come nearer, are two ways of looking at the same fundamental fact. Capital goods may be viewed as *either* accumulated productive power, including the carrying charge, *or* as future utilities discounted in value according to their futurity.

It is to be noted that the capitalization process does not apply to goods which have no durability of service-rendering power, but give up their utilities in an instantaneous act of consumption. That is, the value of such things as food and fuel is not affected by the distribution of their services through time, and is simply the value of the service itself. For this reason, we do not generally distinguish, in the case of such goods, between the goods themselves and their services. The two have absolutely the same value, and as pointed out above, the service cannot be sold separately from the good, as can be done in the case of durable goods by leasing them for a limited time. So it is customary to think of income as made of "goods and services", that is, perishable goods, and the services of persons and of durable goods.

THE NOTION OF ULTIMATE PRODUCTIVE RESOURCES, OR FACTORS OF PRODUCTION: "LAND, LABOR AND CAPITAL." LIMITATIONS OF THIS CLASSIFICATION. The notion of ultimate resources is another case where no single, simple, logical classification can be worked out and followed. It has become traditional to refer to "land, labor, and capital" as the three primary productive factors. Land is used to include everything furnished by nature, and not merely agricultural land. Labor, similarly, includes all human services, skilled and unskilled, and direction as well as execution, though "management" is sometimes given separately as a fourth factor. Capital includes all artificial agencies or produced goods used for further production.

Such a classification of productive agencies has a certain utility, perhaps, in indicating roughly distinct groups, but its serious defects need recognition and emphasis. In the first place, none of the three types is really ultimate; all are largely "produced" as a matter of historical fact. Moreover, it is not clear that one is much more or less original or unproduced than another. What we call natural agencies, as they are used in production, are very different from "raw" nature, untouched and unexamined. Many things have been done to them, many costs incurred in bringing them into use; in fact, averaging out for any large group of natural agencies would probably show that they have cost as much as at any given time they are worth, or in short that their productive value is entirely accounted for by previous expenditure of productive power or "investment", undertaken for much the same motives as any other production of valuable things. Artificial capital goods, on the other hand, are never wholly artificial; at the least, they contain materials furnished by nature. Human beings, too, are essentially products; a human being with no training or culture whatever would have little if any value. The similarity between investment in training and investment in material property has been pointed out. Finally, none of the groups is in any degree homogeneous; there is fully as much difference, for the purposes of economic problems, between different kinds of natural agents, different kinds of capital goods and different kinds of workers as there is between men and machines or either and natural agents, considered as classes.

Two or three general facts more or less on the other side, in favor of the "tripartite" classification, may be briefly stated. The first is that there are good reasons in discussing modern free societies for making a clear distinction between human beings and material productive agencies; the reasons have already been given; human beings are not salable, and are properly regarded as not being "produced", since the investment in them is made under special conditions which do not conform to the economic principles governing the production of property. With regard to the separation between land, or nature, and artificial capital goods, much less of a favorable character can be said. Many economists are dropping this distinction and including land under capital. The real question here, from an economic standpoint, relates to the conditions which regulate the supply of any particular good or agency, namely its durability in use, and the possibility and cost of producing more of it. No doubt in a rough general way the supply of artificial equipment goods as a class is more fully under control than that of natural resources as a class, but there are all degrees within each class. Agricultural fertility can be produced at will, within wide limits, and in the world as a whole new supplies of most kinds of mineral wealth, certainly, remain to be discovered or brought under exploitation which is equivalent to and is production. On the other hand, many artificial goods, direct and indirect, are permanent when once brought into existence. Any useful classification looks forward, not backward; the question of historical origin has no practical significance, except possibly in connection with certain ethical issues. Conditions affecting new supply are different in an old country, whose resources are completely explored and developed, from those of a new country or of the world as a whole. The general character of the classification resulting from drawing the significant distinctions is shown by the table given above, which reveals the complexity of the problem. Land and capital should be thought of, not as groups of concrete things, but as names for elements or qualities in things. The ultimate elements or sources of productive power are *nature, man* and *time,* or *waiting.*

One final remark is in order. The question of a distinction between land and capital must be kept separate from the question of the relation between rent and interest as forms of income. The income derived from either land or capital goods may take the form of either rent or interest, depending on the terms upon which it is received. In explaining the interest rate, it will be brought out that the *"capital"* for which interest is paid and received is neither *capital goods* nor any kind of productive goods as such, but *free productive power,* loaned and borrowed for the purpose of creating or obtaining goods of any kind. When one person hires from another the use of any concrete thing, the payment takes the form of rent. (See Note, page 66).

FREE ENTERPRISE AS A PRICE SYSTEM. THE "WHEEL OF WEALTH." With this long, and perhaps somewhat tedious, but necessary, analysis of the stages in the economic process finally behind us, we may return to the view of economic organization as a system of price relations. Seen in the large, free enterprise is an organization of production and distribution in which the individual or family units get their real income, their "living", by selling productive power for money to "business units" or "enterprises", and buying with the money income thus obtained the direct goods and services which they consume. This view, it will be remembered, ignores for the sake of simplicity the fact that an appreciable fraction of the productive power in use at any time is not really employed in satisfying current wants but to make provision for increased want-satisfaction in the future; it treats society as it would be, or would tend to become, with progress absent, or in a "static" state. It also disregards the organization of activity in other ways than that of free enterprise; the latter is both the most typical and the most complex of the methods of organization in use in modern industrial nations, and the relation to free enterprise of other modes of organization—governmental industry, cooperation, the "handicraft" status (of agriculture, etc.) where the family unit produces and sells a product—is not an especially difficult problem when the working of a system of enterprise is understood. The general character of an enterprise system, reduced to its very simplest terms, can be illustrated by a diagram showing the exchange of productive power for consumption goods between individuals and business units, mediated by the "circulation" of money, and suggesting the familiar figure of the "wheel of wealth". At one point on a circle we have the population as individuals (really families, always) and at the opposite point business enterprises as a group, including all the stages and branches of the productive organization in the broad sense of production which takes in merchandising, finance, etc. The circulation of money is a very literal fact. The upper and lower semi-circles respectively represent the two sets of exchange relations into which each person enters with business in the large, the "sale" of productive power and "purchase" of products. In the final result, it is a single exchange, of productive services for products, with money as an intermediary. It goes without saying that business enterprises consist in the large of the same individuals as "The People" (excluding dependent members of families and wards of the state). Yet it is a mere accident if any individual buys any products at all from the same enterprise to which he sells productive power or of which he is a member in any other capacity.

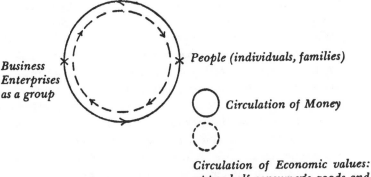

Business Enterprises as a group

People (individuals, families)

Circulation of Money

Circulation of Economic values:
upper half consumer's goods and services
lower half productive services
(labor and use of property)

The nature of a business enterprise presents a problem of considerable subtlety. In its fully developed form it would be entirely separate from those who sell it productive power of any kind. In this theoretically pure form it rarely exists, but its character is approximated by a large modern corporation. The persons who make up or constitute the corporation may not furnish it with any considerable fraction of the personal services or of the material wealth with which it carries on its operations. The work, including that of management, may be performed by persons employed for wages or salaries, from common laborers up to the highest officials, and the property may also be hired from outsiders for a rental or an interest payment. If this were altogether the case, we should have the enterprise of abstract theory. In practice, of course, the men who make up the corporation as a legal entity generally do some of the work of direction and still more commonly furnish some of the property value or "capital" with which it carries on its functions; but in many actual corporations both contributions approach the vanishing point if they do not disappear altogether. The nature of actual enterprises will be sketched somewhat more fully in a later chapter, but detailed discussion belongs to more specialized treatises.

The Economic Organization

It should be noticed that the "money" of the diagram represents the total social income, which takes on four different aspects or meanings at different points in its circular flow. Beginning with its expenditure by individuals for consumption goods and services—(a) on the diagram—it represents to the persons who pay it out the aggregate cost of living; to the enterprise to which it is paid (b) it is business receipts or income. As the enterprises pay it out for productive services it is (c) business expense or cost of producing goods, and to the individuals who receive it for the productive services it is (d) personal (or family) income, in the form of rent, interest and wages, or salaries, according to the kind of productive service and the terms on which the latter is sold.

The study of the price system narrows down to analysis of these two sets of prices and the interrelations between them, the prices of consumption goods and the prices of productive services. The two sets together control the process of production and distribution under free enterprise. Those individuals who do not sell productive power, but use their own labor, or property, or both, in making a product, with or without hiring the service of other persons or their property in addition, do not enter directly into the second of the two markets, but their position is not essentially changed by this fact. In effect they hire their own services from themselves, and their economic status is still determined by the total social situation. Those who render personal services, such as lawyers, doctors, etc., are especially likely to "work for themselves" yet increasingly such persons also are "employed" by an institution or corporation of some kind.

PRICES AND THE TASKS OR FUNCTIONS OF ORGANIZATION. We shall now take up in slightly greater detail the manner in which the economic process is controlled by the two sets of prices. The four main tasks or aspects of organized activity are, as will be remembered, (1) to set standards for determining what things shall be produced and in what proportions, (2) to allocate resources to the various branches of production and combine or coordinate them effectively in each, (3) to distribute the product, and (4) to provide for maintenance and progress.

1. THE FORMULATION OF STANDARDS FOR THE CONTROL OF PRODUCTION. Under the system of free enterprise the first task is most obviously a matter of price, since it is precisely the prices of consumption goods and services which constitute the social measure of their importance. It is through its price that any good exerts the "pull" which assigns productive power to creating it. As we shall repeatedly emphasize, the price measure is not a true index of social importance according to any recognized ethical standard, but it is the one in terms of which production is actually guided, insofar as the principles of free enterprise apply without "social interference" of any kind.

Prices also perform in the short run that special but highly important function essentially the reverse of the above, namely that of adjusting consumption to production during the interval within which the supply cannot be changed.

2. THE ORGANIZATION OF PRODUCTION. Next after the problem of indicating the channels of greatest demand is the two-fold one of making production follow those channels, and of making it "efficient". This second task may be regarded as social business management. It covers (a) the allocation or assignment of productive resources, human and material, to the different lines of industry and (b) their effective *coordination* and direction. The latter, again, includes the location and lay-out of plants, selection of technical processes, determination of the scale of operations, marketing methods, internal personnel organization, and all matters affecting productive efficiency. In the control of production, the two sets of prices work together. Every enterprise is in competition, as explained in the first pages of this chapter, with other enterprises, both in the sale of products and in the purchase of productive services, labor, materials, etc. Each enterprise buys productive services and sells a product or products. The price it can secure for the latter is one factor in determining the price it can pay for the former, the other

factor being the efficiency of the enterprise in converting productive power into products. It is the prices offered for the productive services which actually determine their entry into the industries where demand is greatest and into the establishments within any industry which have the highest efficiency. But the prices of productive services reflect the prices of the products into which they ultimately flow. The precise relation between the prices of particular products and the prices of particular services which combine in infinitely various ways in the making of infinitely various products, constitutes the price problem, which will form the subject of the next two chapters.

3. DISTRIBUTION. The manner in which the product of industry is distributed among the members of society has already been indicated. Each responsible individual sells some productive service or services to some enterprise, or enterprises, and thereby obtains a money income, with which he buys products for consumption from various enterprises— (from "dealers" who buy them from the "producers" as the business world uses the term). It is evident that the share in the final produce which anyone is able to secure depends on (a) the amount of his *money income* and (b) its *purchasing power* over the goods which he desires to consume. But the first of these is determined by the prices of the productive services which he sells to industry, and the second is a matter of the prices of consumption goods, so that the shares in distribution are determined by the same two sets of prices already considered. The inter-connection between the prices of final goods and those of productive services in a relation of mutual determination really ties all three of these major functions of organization intimately together; the interaction of the prices in the two markets sets standards, controls production and distributes the produce, and, as just observed, forms the main content of the study of economics.

4. ECONOMIC PROGRESS AND THE PRICE RÉGIME. The discussion of earlier chapters has brought out the fact that progress involves many phases or aspects, which may be

summed up under the three heads of changes in *resources* (as to amount and kind and distribution of ownership), changes in *technology,* including the technique of business organization, and changes in *wants.* Provision for and control over these progressive changes is one of the unescapable tasks of a system of organization. But as we have insisted at various points, modern social organization is a mixture of most of the possible systems or methods, and it has been pointed out, also, that the control of progress is to an especially limited extent within the domain of individual free enterprise and the price forces. The principal connection between the price system and social progress is mediated by the phenomenon of interest on capital. Most forms of progress call for the use of present resources in ways which are not immediately productive and hence are equivalent to the saving and investment of capital for a future return. Insofar, then, as progress is worked out through the price system at all, interest is the price through which control is chiefly exercised. According to the theory of enterprise, interest constitutes the incentive to save and invest, as well as the incentive to direct into the most productive channels the use of capital already saved. How far in fact interest is the effective stimulus to saving is an unsettled question, though there can hardly be doubt as to its significance in drawing accumulated wealth into productive use and into channels which promise larger rather than smaller returns. Interest applies directly to conscious saving and investment, through the medium of "money". In regard to other phases of economic progress, involving self-sacrifice in the present for the sake of the future in indirect and subtle ways, the relation of the price incentive to the course of events is more obscure.

5. CONTROL OF CONSUMPTION IN THE PERIOD OF UNALTERABLE SUPPLY. There is for many commodities a short period within which the supply cannot be changed and the social problem is that of distributing the available supply over the period and among the consumers. The example of the earlier section was that of an agricultural crop. For some commodities, the price system has developed a com-

plicated mechanism of speculative trading which works out the distribution of the supply. For others a less definite and formal procedure takes care of the problem more crudely.

NOTE. (See p. 59). This view of productive resources (pp. 54-59) is the "orthodox" one in modern economics. The writer now holds that it rests on false assumptions. Capital goods are not produced by labor (or labor and "natural agents") without the cooperation of pre-existing capital. And capital goods cooperate in producing their replacements (of the same or different form). Additions to the total capital of an economy are produced jointly by all kinds of existing resources. Thus both the aggregate capital and any one agent produces its own maintenance and eventual replacement, while yielding an annual flow of consumable product (the yield or "interest") "in perpetuity", or until destroyed through net disinvestment.

Capital, then, is not an indirect method of using "other productive factors"; investment does not lengthen a production period; and the role of time in production must be differently interpreted. "Waiting" is involved in the creation of additional capital in and by an economy as a whole; it goes on, and its result yields an income, as long as the economy endures. In a long-run view, both natural agents and laborers have the qualities of capital. The "tripartite" classification is not a final analysis, as there are no "ultimate" productive resources, not previously produced. This is made fairly clear on pages 57ff. and this view fits the treatment of the supply side in distribution and of the interest rate—pages 104-118.

Demand and Supply and Price

It is a trite saying that "price is determined by demand and supply". Like many other facts which "everyone knows", this is true or false according to the interpretation, and unfortunately the correct interpretation is not an easy task. In order to explain price and the way in which price functions as a regulating force in economic life, it has to be understood in several different interpretations. The main difficulty is that, as often happens, causal relationships run in one direction from one point of view and in the other direction from another. A cold day may be "caused" by a wind, but in the large, as everyone knows, the wind is "caused" by the unequal heating effects of the sun. In the case of these terms, demand and supply, there is obviously a sense in which price determines both, while in a different sense it is being determined by them. A satisfactory explanation of price requires drawing several rather careful distinctions between different uses of these words. In particular, it is necessary to distinguish different meanings according to whether immediate or ultimate relations are to be considered, whether price is to be explained from a short-run or a long-run point of view.

PRICE FROM THE STANDPOINT OF DIFFERENT PERIODS OF TIME. The actual price at any given moment of a standard commodity like wheat, whose price is constantly determined by free competitive dealing in an open market, is fixed by speculative traders who typically are neither producers, nor, to any significant extent, consumers of the commodity. They are literally, "middlemen". Neither producers nor consumers have anything to say about the price. The demand and supply which fix what we shall designate as the actual or momentary or speculative price are the buying and selling activities of traders. Yet it is clear that the buying and selling of traders is in a larger view determined by the amounts which the real consumers will buy and which the producers will sell. So that the price which is immediately determined by speculators' demand and supply is finally determined by consumers' demand and producers' supply. But still another distinction is necessary. For the producers cannot change their supply until a minimum period of time has passed—in the case of wheat, a year or more. The supply for any one year is practically fixed at the amount which has been produced. In a longer time, however, producers can change the amount produced, and will do so, according to conditions which affect the profits in their business. From this third point of view, the demand is the consumers' demand and the supply the producers' supply, as before, but over a period of years the supply is under control, whereas with reference to a single year it is not. Again, the supply will be very different according to whether the conditions of production and sale are those of competition or of monopoly. We must attempt to state the different principles and the relations between them, briefly yet with considerable care to be accurate, as there is no other way to avoid confusion. The notion of a market first calls for a few words.

THE MARKET: NOT A PARTICULAR PLACE BUT THE FIELD OVER WHICH PRICE FIXING FORCES OPERATE. THE LAW OF THE MARKET: UNIFORM PRICE. In everyday usage, the term market may refer to a particular place, a town, or even more narrowly, a building. In economics the word means the whole area, often indefinitely defined, within which the buyers and sellers of a commodity come together and fix a common price. The wheat market is practically the world; there is a world price, not absolutely the same all over the world, but closely interconnected. On the other hand, the market for the coal from a particular mine or the brick from a small factory may not extend beyond a few miles. Obviously, the extent of the market depends on two limiting factors, the *cost of transportation of the commodity,* the *difficulty of communication* among potential buyers and sellers.

The most fundamental law of economic science is that in the same market there cannot be two prices on the same commodity at the same time. The reason is apparent. If Mr. A. is selling wheat to Mr. B. at $1.00 a bushel and Mr. C. is selling it to Mr. D. at $1.10, A. and D. will get together at some price intermediate between $1.00 and $1.10, *if they know the situation.* This law is so perfectly typical, in vital respects, of economic laws in general, that we must dwell upon it a little further. The necessity of its truth is obvious, and it is also well known that there are sales at different prices in close proximity to each other all the time! Economic laws, like other scientific laws, state a *tendency,* a result which *would* follow if certain conditions are present. But actual conditions are likely to diverge from those assumed in stating the tendency. It is necessary to an understanding of the phenomena to see clearly both why there is a law and why there are exceptions to it. In this case, the conspicuous cause for discrepancy between the law and the facts in a particular case is found in the condition: *people do not know the facts.* They pay more to one seller than they would need to pay another because of *ignorance.* This is the most important single cause of exceptions to economic laws. It is quite generally true of such laws that they state what "would" happen if persons in some situation were fully cognizant of the situation in acting.

There are other complications in the law of uniform price, also rather typical of economic reasoning. It specifies the "same" commodity. But is wheat in Paris the same commodity as wheat in Chicago? Or is a physically equivalent fountain pen or can of peas with a label which is a guarantee of quality effectively the same commodity as if it has an unknown name? Or is the same loaf of bread the same commodity in a fashionable grocery and in an outlying one in a section inhabited by laborers? These questions suggest the caution necessary in stating and interpreting generalizations regarding economic facts.

DEMAND AND SUPPLY IN A SPECULATIVE MARKET. MOMEN-
TARY PRICE.   The emphasis on more or less imperfect knowledge of the facts on which action is based finds immediate application in interpreting the relation between the short-run and long-run forces in price fixing. It is a familiar matter that speculation rests on uncertainty. The demand of speculative buyers depends on what they *think* the demand of consumers to be, and the supply of speculative sellers depends on what they *think* to be the real supply of the good, in existence or in prospect. The principle according to which the price is fixed is briefly this: Speculators are interested in the future course of prices, and know that price is finally determined by consumers' demand and producers' supply. They also know that the higher the price of a commodity, the less consumers will in general buy, and vice versa, while a higher price stimulates production in the long run, but production cannot be quickly changed. In consequence, we have a law of speculative demand, that the higher the price demanded, the less of the commodity will be taken (and vice versa), and the converse law for speculative supply, namely that the higher the price offered, the more of the commodity will be sold (and vice versa). The law of price follows obviously: *the price in a market will settle at the point at which the amount of the commodity which the buyers will take is equal to the amount which the sellers will sell.*

THE MEANING OF TERMS; SUPPLY IS AMOUNT SUPPLIED BUT
DEMAND IS NOT AMOUNT DEMANDED.   One must be warned against the unfortunate ambiguity of the word demand in everyday usage. It is linguistically correct to say that a rise in price will reduce the "demand". But this is using the word in practically the opposite sense from that of saying that the demand has not decreased unless at the *same* price less can be sold than before. It is much better in economic discussion to adhere to the second meaning. *Demand is the set of conditions determining how much of a commodity can be sold at any price.* In the case of

supply, however, no such confusion arises, and the word can be taken to refer to the actual quantity of a commodity. The demand for a commodity is shown by a schedule or scale, or if one likes, by a curve, which states the amount the market will take at all different prices within the range of possible price fluctuation. Thus in a given state of the demand for wheat in a given area, a certain number of bushels could be sold within a certain period of time at a dollar, a certain smaller number at a dollar-ten, etc. If the demand increased, the number of bushels salable or amount demanded at *each* price will be greater (and vice versa).

CONDITIONS BACK OF SPECULATORS' OFFERS. SHORT-RUN DEMAND, SUPPLY AND PRICE IN CONTRAST WITH MOMENTARY. In farm crops production is periodic, and the supply of a given year is fixed. Most manufactured goods are not subject to such a definite periodicity, but the rate of production is relatively fixed for a considerable time, which amounts to much the same thing. Consequently, with reference to a limited time, a year in the case of a farm crop and other periods for other commodities, the supply is a given physical magnitude. The demand is of the same character as in the momentary view, an inverse relation between the price and the amount that can be sold. Consequently, if the demand for that period is brought into effective contact with the supply for that period, *a price will be set which makes the amount demanded equal to the supply.* This we may call the law of short-run price, or normal market price. It is the function of the speculative market to bring the demand and supply for the period together, as units, as will be more fully explained presently.

THE THEORY OF SHORT-RUN SUPPLY. When a producer has produced a good for sale he usually has to sell it, and will sell it for the most he can get. It is necessary repeatedly to emphasize the negative fact, that the price at a moment or in the short-run does *not* depend on what it has cost to produce the goods, and only to a very limited extent on what it is expected to cost in the future to produce similar goods. Cost affects price only as it affects supply, and at a moment or in the short run it affects supply little or not at all. The true theory of price, from the short-run standpoint, is that in accord with the law of demand, price controls the amount demanded, and the competition of buyers and sellers sets a price at which the amount demanded will be equal to the supply, meaning the amount there is to be sold within the period before a new supply comes on the market. If the producer has any effect on the price in the short-run it is only by holding the goods off the market for his own use; that is, he affects price only as a consumer, and not as a producer, and the consumption of a commodity by the producers of it is usually insignificant in comparison with the total consumption. Moreover, the consumption by producers is likely to follow a law the opposite of that which describes other consumption. If the price of wheat is high, the wheat producers, being prosperous in consequence of the high price, are likely to use more wheat than they would if it were cheap, instead of less. The essential thing is that under competitive conditions neither producer nor consumer has anything to say about price. All that any individual can do is to buy or not buy, sell or not sell, or buy or sell larger or smaller amounts of the commodity, according to the price. The price is set by impersonal forces. If any individual has any real power over the price it is a sure indication that he has to that extent a monopoly.

THE THEORY OF SHORT-RUN DEMAND. UTILITY, DIMINISHING UTILITY, MARGINAL UTILITY.   An enormous amount of discussion has been devoted in economic literature to explaining the law of demand, to showing *why* people generally buy less of a commodity if the price is high than if it is low. It is pointed out as a principle of psychology that wants are satiable, that there is less satisfaction derived from eating the second apple than from eating the first, that in general the more of any commodity a person consumes or acquires, the less he cares about getting additional units or keeping any one unit he already has, and that consequently the more he has, the less money he will pay for another unit, or take for one of those he already has. In connection with the law of uniform price in a market, this does in some sense "explain" the law of demand. The price must be the same for all units and the more units there are to be sold, in a given market in a given time, the lower must be the price in order to dispose of them all. This principle, that the importance of any unit decreases with an increase in the number of units is called *the law of diminishing utility*, and the utility of the last unit of a supply which determines the price at which all the units have to be sold, is called *the marginal utility* of the supply. The principle of utility explains why coal, which is so much more useful in the abstract than gold, sells at a price so much lower, and why such things as air and water, which are essential to life, commonly command no price at all. There are so many units available that any one unit is easily replaced and no one unit can secure a high price in the one case, or any price in the other. The principle is further explained by the scale of decreasingly important uses for which many commodities are employed if the supply increases. It is also to be remembered that if the price rises, many consumers will drop out of the market altogether, either those who care less than others for the commodity, or those who have less money to spend.

The theory of utility may be helpful in understanding the demand law, but is liable to misinterpretation. In particular, it must not be inferred that the price of a commodity will "measure" its marginal utility to consumers generally. This is not true because of differences in purchasing power. A loaf of bread may give an intense satisfaction to a hungry poor man, because he has not money enough to satisfy his wants more completely, while it is consumed unconsciously or despised by the man with a larger income. What is measured by price is the *relative utility* of a commodity in comparison with other things the purchaser might buy with his money.

THE ELEMENTS WHICH MAKE UP CONSUMERS' DEMAND. It is apparent from the facts just pointed out that the demand of any person for any commodity is a product of two factors, his desire to consume that commodity and his purchasing power, the amount of money he has to spend. These together determine the amount he will purchase at any price. But the intensity of his desire for any particular commodity is again a comparative matter. Especially, it depends on the prices at which other commodities are available, and this in two opposite ways. First, if similar goods, forming ready substitutes for wheat, for example, are available at low prices, the consumer will care less about having wheat, his demand for wheat will be lower as shown by the amount he will take at any given price. This is called the *principle of substitution* in consumption. On the other hand, if things used in connection with wheat are available at low prices, the demand for wheat will be increased. If live-stock are cheap, a man may buy wheat to increase his consumption of meat or to keep a saddle horse, when he would not think of buying it for personal use at any price and would not buy at the price he does pay if the other things were dear. This is the *principle of joint demand.* The consumer's problem is to get the greatest possible amount of satisfaction out of the expenditure of his income. Obviously, he will achieve this result by *apportioning his total expenditure among the commodities available in such proportions that the utility purchased by a dollar is the same in the case of every commodity.* If a dollar buys greater utility in one field than another, expenditure should be shifted from the second field to the first. The prices, it must be remembered, are beyond his control, and are not appreciably affected by the action of any one consumer in purchasing or not purchasing any particular commodity. The words italicized state a principle which may be called the *equalization of the margin in consumption.*

Like all economic laws, this principle is subject to reservations. It is not to be assumed that consumers do apportion their expenditures in strict accordance with the principle of equal marginal utilities, or that they carefully strive to do so, or that it would be wise for them to strive more carefully than they do. There is a point where the added satisfaction obtained ceases to be worth the effort of deliberation. There is such a thing as too much taking thought; an "irrational passion for dispassionate rationality" may take much of the joy out of life. Yet the principle is valuable as stating a tendency, and helping to make economic behavior in the large more understandable.

"ELASTICITY"; AN IMPORTANT PROPERTY OF DEMAND. The general law of demand admits of few exceptions, the law namely that the higher the price the less can be sold.[1] But this is much *more* true of some commodities than of others. With some, a small rise in price will cause a large decrease in sales, with others a much smaller decrease. The degree of responsiveness of consumption to price changes is called the "elasticity of demand". In general, *necessities* and such conventional necessities as tobacco, have an *inelastic* demand in comparison with other goods. The larger the income, naturally, the bigger will be the proportion of consumption that is little affected by price changes. In order to have a standard for comparison, a demand is said to be *elastic* if a one per cent change in price causes a change of more than one per cent in the sales, and *inelastic* if the change in sales is less, relatively, than the price change. When the relative change in sales is just equal to that in price, the commodity has a demand of *unitary elasticity*, or the elasticity of its demand is one. This is not quite accurate. Strictly speaking, the elasticity is unity when a change in price causes a change in purchases which just offsets the price change, leaving the money value of the total volume of sales unchanged. Putting the matter the other way around, demand is *elastic* when a given relative change in *supply* causes a smaller relative change in *price*, and conversely for *inelastic* demand.

The question of elasticity of demand is very important in connection with monopoly, and with the prob-

[1] Throughout this discussion of price, a change in price means a change *in comparison with other goods*. A change in *general prices* is a change in the purchasing power of money. The effects of such a change constitute a very special sort of problem, which is reserved for separate treatment and cannot be fully discussed in an introductory book on economics.

lem of taxation. If the demand is elastic, a monopolist cannot raise his price very greatly without losing more through reduction of his sales than he gains by the higher price. And if the demand is elastic, a tax on the commodity will be relatively unproductive, because of the shrinkage in its production and use. It is also a vital factor in agricultural problems. The demand for agricultural products is typically inelastic, and the output subject to uncontrollable fluctuations due to the changes of the weather. In consequence, a large crop causes prices ruinously low to producers, while a short crop burdens the consumer with prices excessively high. If there is some tendency for such a situation to "even up in the long run", this by no means remedies the evil. Such fluctuations make intelligent planning in an industry unduly difficult and are themselves hard to provide against. Unfortunately, the great bulk of the human race is not in a position to wait for things to even up over a period of years; they do not live in the long run, but by stretching their resources almost from day to day.

THE SOCIAL FUNCTION OF PRICE IN THE SHORT RUN, DISTRIBUTION OF AN EXISTING SUPPLY IN TIME AND SPACE. It was pointed out in an earlier chapter, in enumerating the functions or tasks of organization, that the general function of co-ordinating production and consumption commonly takes on opposite aspects in the short-run and the long-run views. In the long run, it is obviously a question of making production conform to consumption standards. But due to the time which is usually required for changing production, the short-run problem is that of distributing the existing supply, or that forthcoming during the interval of adjustment, over the time for which it has to suffice and among all individuals and groups in the market. In the system of free enterprise or "price system" it is price which has to perform both these functions. The way in which price acts to control production will be explained presently. It is obvious without extended explanation that the price, the costliness of goods to consumers, prevents their wasting goods available in stocks, such as wheat after harvest, and bringing on destitution or scarcity later. It also operates to keep any particular consumer or group of consumers from using the supply to excess and depriving others of their share.

The manner in which price performs this twofold distribution is not indeed the ideal way, especially as regards the second part of it or the distribution among consumers. In regard to the first part, the distribution of consumption over the interval, there is little to be said by way of objection. The tendency of competition is to maintain a uniform price throughout the period, with allowance for the cost of storing the unused supply, as will be explained further in the next section. If the income of the consumers is uniform over the period—and there is no reason to believe that it will be otherwise except for chance variations—this should lead to the "correct" distribution of the consumption. With respect to distribution among consumers, however, a different verdict has to be rendered. Competition likewise sets a uniform price for all purchasers, which means that a limited supply of a commodity will be divided among them in proportion to their pecuniary demand, as already defined, the resultant of desire and the purchasing power. But with the inequality in the distribution of purchasing power, i.e., money income, which we find in modern society, the burden of any considerable scarcity of an important commodity falls so excessively upon the poor that the results of unregulated competition become indefensible. When an abnormal scarcity occurs, the government is forced to intervene and establish some limitations on the consumption of the well-to-do, as was done in the case of sugar and fats during the World War. Moreover, the ordinary normal situation is only less acute, and we know that the public authority and private charity are constantly acting to secure to no small fraction of the population a minimum supply of the essentials of life which they are unable to procure for themselves.

THE THEORY OF SPECULATION: THE RELATION BETWEEN MOMENTARY AND SHORT-TIME PRICE. It was stated in the previous section that the tendency of free competition is to maintain a uniform price during a period which must be covered by a limited supply, with allowance for costs of storage. This is the function of the much-abused institution of speculation—abused partly because it is misunderstood and partly because, like other economic institutions and processes, it does not always work in accord with its general theory. The social desirability of the result, i.e., of a uniform price modified only by storage costs, has been commented upon. It can be briefly shown that free speculation does tend to bring about this result. A little consideration of the case of wheat will make this clear. If the price of wheat right after harvest is below the point at which the existing supply will cause it to remain constant until the next harvest, that is, if it is below the theoretical short-time or normal market price, then wheat will tend to be consumed at a more rapid rate than it would be if the price were at the correct point. This must result in a comparative shortage later in the season, which must raise the price correspondingly above the correct level. In this situation, anyone who can discern the facts can obviously make money for himself by buying wheat and holding it for the rise. Conversely, if at any time the price is above the point at which demand and supply will keep it constant, money can be made by "selling short", that is, by contracting to deliver wheat in the future at the ruling price, for when the price goes down, as it must, the seller can buy the wheat to fulfill his contract for less than he received for it.

This possibility of making money out of price changes sets men to work to procure the most accurate information obtainable in regard to the existing conditions of demand and of supply and to make the most accurate possible forecast of future prices. But whenever a speculator buys wheat for a rise he tends to raise the price at the time he buys and will lower it at some future time, whenever he thinks it advantageous to sell, thus reducing the range of the price change of which he seeks to take advantage. And conversely, if speculators are offering to contract wheat for future delivery at a price below the current price, this tends to stimulate the actual owners of wheat, the producers, to sell, and to make the consumers hold off from purchasing, which actions must bring down the current price. Thus speculation operates to set the price at any time at exactly the point at which the purchases of consumers will make the supply just last out the season. Of course the speculator, or anyone who holds wheat from one part of the period to another, expects to recoup the storage costs, which therefore tend to modify purchases and sales enough to make the price go up during the season by just enough to cover them.

Most of the popular abuse of speculators is due to failure to understand the function they perform, and especially the failure to see that they can only make money by doing what is to the interest of producers and consumers alike to have them do. Moreover, if all speculators judge correctly, no money will be made in speculation, except payment at fair rates for the trouble involved in performing the service. And finally, it is a fact demonstrable by statistical investigation that speculators as a class do not make more than that. The notion that they fix prices arbitrarily is false; an individual trader normally has very little more influence on the price than an individual producer or consumer. False also is the impression that prices are usually low after harvest and go up later, giving the middleman a huge profit. The fact is that on the average prices of grain crops dealt in on speculative markets do not go up during the season enough to pay the cost of holding them over, and speculative middlemen as a group lose rather more than they gain. The reason for this is, no doubt, that the "game" they play is much like gambling and has a similar psychology, which leads them to overreach themselves somewhat. It is not easy to see how organized speculation could be prevented, and if it were, the result would be that producers and consumers would have to make their own estimates, and buy and sell accordingly, which would be far more costly and lead to much more inaccurate results. The real evils of speculation are due to "manipulation" through misrepresentation of facts by fraudulent reports and the like, and to the operations of ignorant persons whose mere gambling on the market often produces serious effects.

The Economic Organization

DEMAND AND SUPPLY IN THE LONG RUN. LONG-TIME NORMAL
PRICE.   In the short run, supply is fixed, and consumption must be controlled with reference to it. In the long
run, supply is under control of the price forces, and
adapts itself to the conditions of demand. To be sure,
perfect adaptation of supply to demand conditions would
eliminate the practical difference between the two points
of view; but demand may change quickly and supply
slowly; or supply, in many lines, such as agriculture, may
vary from causes beyond control, and in other lines as a
result of miscalculation, so that in fact the two modes of
adjustment are usually going on at the same time. Speculators are striving for purely selfish reasons to act in a way
which will in fact set a price which will control consumption at the socially desirable rate with reference to the
existing supply. At the same time, producers strive to act
(for purely selfish reasons) in a way which will in fact
yield such supplies of goods that prices will tend to be
uniform from one season or production period to another as well as uniform throughout a given production
period, and that consumption will be set at a level determined by the economical use of existing productive
resources and not merely at a level determined by the
economical use of existing supplies of goods. This is the
significance of the long-run price adjustment. The precise meaning of the "economical" use of productive resources will be discussed later; as in the case of the distribution of an existing supply through competitive
buying and selling, it is not necessarily an ideal arrangement in a social or ethical sense.

DEMAND IN THE LONG RUN IS CONSUMERS' DEMAND. A RATE
OF CONSUMPTION DEPENDENT UPON PRICE.   The long-run
meaning of demand is not greatly different from the
short-run meaning. It is consumers' demand, the resultant
of desire and purchasing power, the former relative to
the desire for other commodities which may compete
with or complement the one in question. The only difference is that long-run demand is defined as a *rate* of
purchasing at different prices, so many units per day or
week or year, right along at one price, and so many at

another, instead of a certain absolute number within a fixed period. The "law", too, is the same as before, and for the same reason—the principle of diminishing utility; the higher the price of any good, the less of it will be sold in the year or other unit of time.

SUPPLY IN THE LONG RUN: RATE OF PRODUCTION DEPENDENT UPON PRICE. THE LAW OF LONG-TIME NORMAL PRICE. In the long run, the amount of any commodity which will be put on the market bears some determinate relation to the price which can be obtained for it. This hardly calls for proof. A complete explanation of the relation between the price and the amount which will be produced, will indeed require some time, but the fact that there is a connection is all that is required here. It is not necessary to assume that the connection is always a direct one, that the higher the price, the more of the good will be produced, though this is no doubt the general case. Except for the special definition of demand and supply, the argument is the same as in the previous views of price. Price controls amount demanded and amount supplied, and the price which competition tends to set is that which will make these two amounts equal. It is to be remembered always that long-run normal price is hypothetical, a theoretical tendency, not an actuality. Price is always fixed by momentary speculative demand and supply, but tends always to move consumption and production, and to be moved by demand and production into a position and a relation where consumption, production and price will be stable, or in "equilibrium" (the "demand" proper and the fundamental conditions of production being given and unchanged).

THEORY OF LONG-RUN SUPPLY UNDER COMPETITIVE CONDITIONS. PRICE AND COST. Supply must be discussed separately for competition and monopoly, though it will be shown that there is not the sharp distinction between the two that is commonly assumed. Only farm products and a few standard, staple things are produced and sold under the condition of approximately perfect competition. The test of effective competition is that the producer has nothing to say about price, except to produce or not produce, or produce more or less of the good at the price set by the market, which anyone must be free to do. If there is any artificial barrier to prevent anyone producing and selling the good who chooses to do so, the fact is proof that monopoly exists; likewise if any producer is in a position to have a "price policy" the fact proves that he possesses monopoly power. Manifestly a wheat producer cannot discuss price. He takes the market price, or, if he insists on a fraction of a cent more, he does not sell his wheat. The producer of a manufactured article nearly always has more or less monopoly power, since no other producer is producing exactly the same commodity.

The producer, whether an individual owner of a small business or the manager of a large corporation, is out to make money. His function is to hire productive services ("land, labor and capital") in the market in competition with other producers, use them to make a product and sell the product in the market in competition with other producers. We can speak as if a single enterprise carried on the entire process of producing any commodity, from ultimate resources to the good or service ready for consumption. Division of the process into stages performed by different enterprises, some of which buy or sell or both buy and sell intermediate goods or partial products does not affect the principles involved, and neither does the character of the marketing organization at either end of the productive process. The money which the producer pays out for productive power ("rent, wages and interest") constitutes his cost of production, and the money he receives for his product is his gross income. Anything that he makes as income for himself is the difference between the two amounts, or what is loosely called "profit". In conformity with the nature of economic laws as statements of tendency, based on the assumption that men know what they are doing and act in accord with economic motives, the theory of normal price assumes that goods will be produced whenever they can be produced at a profit, and will not be produced when production involves a loss. That is, whenever an industry is profitable, it will tend to expand and whenever it is unprofitable it will tend to shrink, until the "profit" represents only payment at the going rates for whatever the producer himself puts into the enterprise in the way of personal effort or use of property. This minimum amount of "profit" is treated in economic discussion as a part of the cost of production and separated from "pure profit", which includes anything in excess of necessary profit and also any deficiency, any loss.

The obvious conclusion of this reasoning is the familiar principle that *price tends to equal cost of production*. It is commonly stated in the form that cost of production "determines" price, but this is not true without considerable qualification. In the first place, as already stated, cost of production has very little to do with price at any given time, after the goods have been produced or their production irrevocably determined upon. The relation of cost to price is always that of setting a standard toward which price will tend in the future to conform, and of course it is expected future costs and not actual present or past costs which do even this. Second, the relation between cost and price is indirect; cost affects price only as it affects the supply—the amount produced and offered for sale—and is entirely independent of cost. Finally, the relation between cost and price is one of *mutual* causality, as will presently be shown.

THE VARIATION OF COST AS OUTPUT VARIES. What really fixes price is output, supply, in relation to demand, cost acting only indirectly by determining output, as explained. Thus it becomes a fundamental question as to how cost is affected by changes in output. In some industries, certainly, increasing output will not greatly affect the cost, per unit, of producing the commodity. Such an industry is said to be subject to "constant" cost. In others, certainly, increasing output will involve increasing cost per unit. This seems to be the "natural" case, since increased output involves increased demand for the productive services used in the industry, and this increase in demand will tend to raise their prices, and these prices are the costs of production. Such an industry is one of "increasing cost", and "constant cost" industries are those in which the increase in cost with increasing output is negligible because the industry as a whole does not appreciably affect the total demand for any productive resource or raw material which it uses. In still other industries, it is commonly held that an increase in output is coupled with a decrease in cost per unit. This is supposed to result from the more economical methods of production which are practicable when the scale of operations is larger. It seems probable, however, that these "economies of large-scale production" are not only much exaggerated in the popular mind, but that when they are present they tend to bring about a concentration of the industry in larger and larger units, ending in the establishment of monopoly. At least, a considerable number of writers on economics, in addition to the writer of this book, are skeptical as to whether an industry is likely to show both a condition of decreasing cost and a condition of stable competition. If the industry becomes a monopoly, the relation between cost and price follows a different law, as will be shown in a later section. In any case, if cost does decrease with increasing output, a point must come at which price decreases more rapidly, so that the two come together. Otherwise the production would expand indefinitely.

THE ULTIMATE MEANING OF COST. THE DOUBLE RÔLE OF COST IN REGULATING PRODUCTION. To the producer or entrepreneur, cost of production represents the *payments* for productive power, or for materials which embody productive power and in paying for which he really pays for productive power previously expended upon them. To society, the cost of producing a certain supply of a commodity must have a different meaning, since in all payments and transfers what one gives up another gets, leaving society as a whole neither richer nor poorer than before. The meaning of cost to society will be made clear if we consider the reasons why the producer must make his payments and the causes which determine the amount he must pay in any instance.

Productive power has value to producers only for use in producing goods which can be sold for a price. The price which any producer will pay—can be made to pay—depends on the price which he can obtain for the products which result from the use of the productive power. The price he does pay—has to pay—is practically determined by the competition of other producers bidding against him for the same productive power he buys. To the owner from whom productive power is bought, it may have value for other purposes than the production of goods to sell, and indeed commonly does. In the case of labor particularly, the worker would often—not always—prefer to use his time and strength in other ways than producing salable goods, and would do so if it were not for the money inducement to do otherwise. The same may be true, and is more or less true, of the other productive factors. The owner of land could use it for playgrounds and ornamental effects of various sorts, and the owner of capital could find similar uses for his resources. In general, however, these considerations have little indeed to do with fixing the amounts actually paid and received for the use of any of the productive agencies, even of labor. The statement holds that their remuneration is determined by their competitive value for productive use. Entrepreneurs compete against each other in purchasing them, and the one who is able to pay the most gets them in each case. If competition is effective there will be a number of entrepreneurs in approximately equal position as to ability to pay, and the successful bidder will have to go to his limit to get the service.

Now the competition of producers in buying productive power is of two sorts, or takes place in two fields, which it is important to keep separate and properly related. Every producer has in bidding to meet (1) the competition of producers in other industries, making other products, and (2) the competition of other producers in the same industry, making the same product. Thus his ability to compete depends on two considerations, (1) the price obtainable for his product in comparison with other products involving the use of the same forms of productive power, and (2) the amount of product he is able to put on the market through the use of a given amount of productive power, in comparison with other producers in the same industry, or in other words the efficiency of his organization.

It will be clear that these two elements in the ability of any producer to outbid his rivals in securing productive power are connected with two socially vital considerations in connection with the economic system as a whole. The first element, that the producer of the more valuable commodity can outbid the producer of the less valuable, provides the mechanism by which the competitive form of social organization guides the apportionment of productive power among different uses. As previously explained, price is competitive society's measure of the importance of different means of want-satisfaction. The competition of entrepreneurs tends to attract productive power into the field of making any commodity or service as long as it is worth more for that use than any other, and to divert it to some other use at the point where the other use becomes the more valuable, in terms of the price measure. The second element in the competitive buying power of producers enables the more efficient producer of a particular product to outbid the less efficient, and constitutes the competitive system's provision for guaranteeing the most effective possible use of resources. Thus the two elements together provide for the accomplishment of the second of the primary functions of organization (the twofold function of allocation and co-ordination). Given the price measure of the relative importance of different uses of power, the competition of producers for productive power tends to guide or force productive power into the most important use, and to force the employment of the most efficient available productive technique—and incidentally, to encourage the development of constantly more effective technique as well. At the same time, the payments for productive power which are "costs" to producers are "income" to those who receive them; they constitute the consumers' purchasing power, and it is by means of them that the competitive system performs the third great task of organization, namely distribution. But the fact that productive power exists in different forms—not merely "land, labor and capital" but innumerable kinds of each—which forms are complementary in use, gives rise to a special problem in connection with the pricing of them individually and this problem must be postponed to another chapter.

THE RELATION OF MUTUAL CAUSALITY BETWEEN COST AND PRICE. PRICE-DETERMINING AND PRICE-DETERMINED COSTS. The twofold competition which determines the cost to any producer of productive power for producing a product—the competition, that is, of other industries and of other producers in the same industry—gives rise to two different relations between price and cost. Some forms of productive power, such as unskilled labor and free capital funds, are used in practically every industry, while other forms such as skilled labor and most types of machinery, are practically specialized to the making of some one product. It is evident that in the pricing of the latter type, competition of other industries is inoperative, and the price of such productive services merely reflects the value of that particular product only. Payments for such specialized services, determined only by competition among producers making the same product, are properly regarded as "price-determined" costs.

On the other hand, the price paid for an unspecialized productive service is to a negligible extent determined by the value of any one product; what it costs in any one industry is mainly a reflection of what it is worth in other industries. In this case, where the payment which must be made is independent of the price of the product, it acts to determine that price, through affecting the amount produced as already explained. Such costs are "price-determining". It should be understood that in reality it is the price of the competing products, acting through the prices of productive power, which regulates the supply and price of any one product. The prices of productive power are always derived from the prices of products as a group; but with regard to any one product, the cost seems to determine the price. The effect of one product on the value of the productive power is negligible in comparison with the mass of all other products for which it is used.

The Economic Organization

DIMINISHING UTILITY AND DIMINISHING RETURNS. The rôle of diminishing utility in connection with production will be apparent. The more of any commodity is produced, the smaller becomes the utility of any unit to the buying public, and in consequence, the lower becomes the price at which the commodity must be sold. Meanwhile, production of more of one commodity means the production of less of others, and the utility, and price, of the others increases. In so far as price is a measure of utility, the tendency is to use the existing stock of social productive resources to create a maximum total of utility, in the same way that a consumer uses his income to buy a maximum total of utility, in a market where various commodities are offered at a given price. As was observed before, price is by no means a correct measure of the real, social importance of goods. For, in the first place, the preferences of individuals, reflected in their price offers, do not always represent what is "best" for the individuals themselves. And in the second place, the vast differences in the amounts of money which different buyers have to spend still less reliably indicate differences in the importance to society of those individuals or others dependent upon them. Moreover, the purchase and consumption of commodities not infrequently affects, in many ways, for good and for ill, other persons than those who do the buying and consuming. As with all other economic laws, it is equally necessary here to understand the principle, as representing a general tendency to direct productive power into channels of greatest social usefulness, and to understand the conditions which make for numerous and important exceptions to that tendency. Some of the reasons for the great inequality, and inequity in the inequality, of the distribution of purchasing power, will be made clearer in the next chapter. The diminishing importance, or remunerativeness, of productive power, as more and more of it is used in the production of any single commodity, resulting from the diminishing utility and price of the commodity produced, is *one phase* of a principle called *the law of diminishing returns,* another phase of which will be brought out in the discussion of distribution. Diminishing returns, in the phase which is now being discussed, is evidently but another name for increasing cost: a decrease in the value produced by a unit of resources is coupled with an increase in the value of the resources used in producing a unit of product, the increased value of the resources reflecting the increased value of some competing product for which they might be used.

THE RELATION BETWEEN SHORT-RUN PRICE AND LONG-RUN NORMAL PRICE. PRODUCTION AS WELL AS MARKETING INVOLVES SPECULATION. In concluding this discussion of long-time normal price let us repeat that it represents the *tendency* of the competitive adjustments taking place at any particular time. Normal price, with normal production and consumption (production and consumption being equal, of course, in a long-run view) is the condition which *would* be brought about if the existing state of the technical arts and organization, and the existing demand, were to remain unchanged long enough, free from accidental disturbances, for production to be brought to its final adjustment in relation to demand. The force which tends to adjust production to demand is the profit-seeking motive of individual producers, and the chief interfering cause which prevents a perfect adjustment is *error* on the producers' part. Producers cannot accurately know the conditions of demand in the present, and still less can they know the demand of the future time to which their present plans and activities relate. Under modern methods, the process of producing goods extends over a *long period of time* from the first preparations until the product is ready for the market. Furthermore, their activities are affected by causes more or less beyond the possibility of accurate prediction and control—notably in the case of agriculture. The situation is aggravated by the fact that one enterprise turns out but a small fraction of the total supply of its product, and that one producer does not know what others are planning to do, and they cannot act as a unit. All these considerations work to introduce a large element of *risk* into producers' activities.

The manager, like the speculator, is attempting to forecast the future, and as in the case of the speculator, those who are more successful in their forecasts, whether from shrewdness or luck, make money, and the others lose. And, again as in the case of speculation in the market, the man whose prediction is correct and who makes money for himself, is the one who is acting in harmony with the social interest in so far as that interest is reflected by pecuniary demand. He makes money by producing the goods most in demand at the time they come on the market. The motive upon which competitive society relies to attract productive power into the most desirable use is the higher price-offer on the part of producers in that field. The motive which leads producers to make the right price-offers is the desire to make a *profit* and avoid a *loss*. Business management involves two main types of activity, of which this matter of forecasting conditions is one and the selection of methods is the other, and the forecasting of demand is the more difficult and important task. A little reflection will show a still further resemblance between management and speculation on a produce exchange. That is that money is made, not only by doing what society's interest requires to have done, but at the expense of those who do otherwise. If all the producers were to forecast correctly, there would be no profits, and no losses! In that event the short-time price would always coincide with the long-time price, just as the momentary price would always coincide with the short-time price if speculators in the market bought and sold on the basis of perfectly correct estimates. In the "correct" adjustment, managers would just get fair wages for their efforts, as in the "correct" adjustment traders on the exchange would do.

MONOPOLY AND COMPETITION. A DEGREE OF MONOPOLY, WITH COMPETITION THROUGH SUBSTITUTION, THE MOST COMMON SITUATION. Some reference has already been made, in the earlier part of this chapter, to the relation between monopoly and competition. It was pointed out that only standardized commodities like the leading grains, which are marketed on an impersonal basis, exemplify completely competitive conditions. Goods in a form ready for consumption are typically marketed on a personal basis;

the consumer knows whose product he is buying, and there is more or less distinction between the goods of one producer and the "same" commodity put out by another. In all such cases, the producer has more or less freedom in setting a price (whereas the wheat producer has none at all) and this is to say that he has more or less monopoly. He has a monopoly of the name under which he sells his goods and of whatever differences really distinguish his product from that of others, including whatever the name may mean in the way of guarantee of quality, auxiliary services in connection with the goods, etc.

It should be apparent that the crux of the whole matter, as between monopoly and competition, is the *degree* of distinction between the goods of one producer and those of other producers. In the case of wheat, there is no distinction, and no monopoly, or in other words competition only (though the term "perfect" competition is used to signify more than the mere absence of monopoly). The seller of a branded good, practically identical physically with the goods of other makers, such as Portland cement or flour, has a small element of monopoly. If there is a real physical difference between the goods as in automobiles for example, the element of monopoly is correspondingly greater. Thus it is clearly a matter of degree whether a particular business is classed as monopolistic or competitive. The Ford Company has a monopoly of *Ford* cars, but not of cars; the makers of "Ivory" soap have a monopoly of *Ivory* soap, but not of soap, and so on. Either certainly faces real *competition* from other cars and other soaps. No line can be drawn between monopoly and competition. An automobile competes with other means of transportation as well as other cars, and a soap competes with other solvents and cleansers as well as other soaps.

Ultimately all commodities compete with each other for the consumer's money. In fact, the relation is much closer than is generally recognized. Food products compete directly with automobiles *in the same use,* in so far as each is purchased to maintain social position or make a display, which none will deny is the fact in large measure. There can hardly be such a thing as absolute monopoly, production freed entirely from competition. Outside a certain undefined range of similarity, partly determined by the accident of names, competition is more commonly called substitution; and perfect substitution, or interchangeability, is perfect competition. In this sense, competition is universal; every commodity has substitutes, in some sense—unless it is water, in places where that is a commodity. By the same reasoning, no commodity (except water) is really "necessary". Much confusion results from thinking of food and clothing as necessary commodities; we have to have food and clothing, but we do not have to have any particular food or article of clothing which is a commodity on the market.

ELASTICITY OF DEMAND THE TEST OF MONOPOLY POWER. It has already been stated that ability to fix price measures the degree of monopoly power. Another way of saying the same thing is that elasticity of demand is the test and measure. The demand for the product of a single producer in a fully competitive industry, a single wheat farmer for instance, is infinitely elastic. The least change in the price asked will change his possibility of selling from zero to an indefinite amount. As the degree of uniqueness of the product increases, or the facility of substituting competing products decreases, the elasticity of demand falls off, and with decreased responsiveness of sales to price change, monopoly power increases. In conformity with what was just said about necessaries, inelasticity of demand is chiefly a matter of convention and habit. Substitution is possible, but it "isn't done". Another cause of inelasticity is complementarity in use with something much more costly than the article itself. The consumption of phonograph needles or Ford parts will be practically independent of their price, within wide limits.

THE NATURE OF MONOPOLY. THE EVILS INVOLVED. The word monopoly comes from two Greek words meaning "one" and "merchant", i.e., only one seller of a commodity. What is meant by a commodity, or the basis for classifying the products of two enterprises as different commodities, is a matter of large uncertainty, as already pointed out. An enterprise is not thought of as a monopoly unless it is in a position to charge a price above that at which other persons could produce an equivalent commodity, and would do so if not prevented by some special barrier. The nature of the barrier determines the kind of monopoly in the customary classification. The barrier, in the case of the old monopolies, in connection with which the word was first used, was the law. Rulers granted monopolies as gifts to favorites, or sold them to raise revenue. This kind of monopoly is represented today by the patent right given an inventor, copyright on books, etc., though these are established as a matter of social policy. It is called a "legal" monopoly. No exhaustive classification of monopolies will be attempted here. A legal monopoly may be retained by the government itself to raise revenue when it is called a "fiscal monopoly", or it may be retained to control the consumption of the commodity, or for other reasons, and given other names. The term "natural monopoly" is in general use, but refers to a number of different situations. The most common is that of industries such as gas and water works which require a fixed investment to serve a given market which it would involve enormous waste to duplicate. Another important class is that sometimes called "capitalistic" monopolies, in which the barrier preventing competition is the threat of "unfair" competition of some sort.

The outstanding evil of monopoly is of course the burden under which it places the consumer of paying a higher price for the commodity than is necessary, and allowing the owner of the monopoly an unearned income—if it *is* unearned. A less conspicuous evil, but one which may be more serious, is the reduction in the use of the good. For this and other reasons our patent system is a crude and wasteful way of rewarding inventors. When the price of any good is artificially raised, productive power is diverted from the production of that commodity to the production of others having a lower utility as measured by price—in addition to the diversion of production from satisfying other wants of consumers to satisfying those of the owner of the monopoly.

93

Monopolists often try, with more or less success, to practice a policy which to some extent reduces this second evil, though that is not the reason they do it. This is the device of *class price*, that is, charging different consumers different prices, in accordance with their ability or willingness to pay rather than do without the good. Another method is to rent the monopolized good and charge in proportion to the amount it is used instead of selling it outright. This can be done by selling supplies for it at a monopoly price. Both these devices, as noted, really reduce the harm done by the monopoly, but they arouse more violent resentment than the direct method of exploitation, and have in some cases been outlawed in the United States. The outstanding example of class price is the practice on the part of the railroads of charging for transporting freight "what the traffic will bear", in accordance with a complicated classification.

THE THEORY OF MONOPOLY PRICE. EFFECTS OF TAXATION. Under conditions of competition the production of a commodity tends to be carried to the point where the price is equal to the cost of production, including payment for the producer's own services as well as those which he hires from other persons. When an industry is profitable, it tends to expand until it is no longer so. The producers in it as a group, lose money of course, by the expansion; but they do not act as a group, if they compete, but as individuals; and any individual gains by increasing production, for his addition to output makes no appreciable difference in the price—and if he does not increase output someone else will.

With Monopoly, all this is different. The monopolist does act as a unit. And it can be shown by mathematical reasoning of a fairly simple character that it is always profitable to a monopolist to stop production more or less short of the point of eliminating profit. This is true when his demand is most elastic, and more true the less elastic the demand. The precise point at which production will be stopped depends on the nature of the variation of cost and selling price when total output varies, but the principle is always the same. The less the monopolist produces, the higher the price per unit he can secure. There is always a point at which the loss in number of units sold offsets gain from increased price, leaving a maximum total net profit. The monopolist strives to find that point and produce that amount. Under monopoly as under competition, the price depends upon the amount produced and marketed, and the only way in which the monopolist can control price is by limiting the supply.

A tax on a monopoly may or may not cause the monopolist still further to restrict output and raise price and in this sense pass a part of the tax on to the consumer, or in technical language "shift" it. It depends on the manner in which the tax is levied. If it is a lump sum on the business as a unit, such as a license fee, it obviously will not affect the size of supply which it is most profitable to produce, or the price, and such a tax will be borne by the producer. The same is true of a tax levied as a percentage of the monopoly profit itself. A tax of a fixed amount on each unit of output, however, will cause the maximum profit point to correspond to a smaller supply and higher price than if the tax had not been levied. Such a tax will cause an additional burden to the consumer. There is no definite relation, however, between the increase in the amount paid by consumers as a group for the good and the amount of the tax, and the monopolist himself may also be affected in different ways under different conditions of demand and of cost. Normally, he will incur a loss from the reduced consumption of his product as well as from having finally to bear a larger or smaller part of the tax.

Distribution: The Pricing of Productive Services Individually

Our discussion of the long-run price of goods and services used directly in the satisfaction of wants has shown that the tendency is for such prices to equal the "costs of production". It is also emphasized that the costs of production are the payments for productive power, and that these payments, which are *costs* from the producer's point of view are *income* to those who receive them and in fact constitute the principal medium by which the product of industry is distributed among individuals and families. The only other legitimate income in a competitive society is that of the producers themselves, or *profit* (including the gains of professional speculators); the relation of profit to income received as the price of productive power sold in the market will be taken up after an explanation has been given of the forces which determine these prices.

THE PROBLEM OF DISTRIBUTION; JOINT DEMAND; THE APPORTIONMENT OF PRODUCT VALUE AMONG DIFFERENT FACTORS CO-OPERATING IN CREATING IT. To say that price tends to be equal to cost of production is to say that the money value of productive power tends to be equal to the money value of its product. That fact is the starting point of the theory of distribution. It goes without saying that the ground on which persons receive legitimate income in economic society is the furnishing of productive power to industry, or by gift from some person who does receive it from that source. The total income of society is apportioned in some way among the persons who furnish the total productive power, including managers and owners of enterprises, and the total income of any establishment or enterprise is also apportioned in some way among those who furnish productive power to that enterprise, including the owners and managers. The problem which remains is that of explaining the mechanism and the process of this apportionment.

It will be evident that the problem of distribution arises altogether out of the fact that different kinds of productive agencies or productive power work together in the creation of any single product—and practically out of the further fact that these different kinds of productive agencies belong to and are furnished by different persons. If only one kind of productive power were used in creating any one product, there would be no place for a theory of distribution, beyond the theory of normal price already given. The apportionment or allocation of any kind of productive power among its different uses and among different users in each industry, and the tendency of competition to make the value of the productive power equal to the value of the product in the most productive and most economical use would be all there would be to say about the pricing of productive power. Even the much discussed question as to which "caused" the other, price of product or price of productive power, would be under these conditions a rather obviously otiose one. The prices of all the products for which any kind of productive power was used and the price of that kind of productive power would be in a system of mutual causation, like the level of the water in a set of intercommunicating tanks. The level of the water in any one tank might be said to be "caused" by the level in all the others; the level in any one tank would correspond with the price of one product, and the common level in all of them would correspond with the price of the productive service. If any kind of productive agency were only usable in the creation of some one product, and not distributed among a number, its price would be "caused" by the price of that product only.

In the real world, the facts are different from this simple imaginary situation. It is most exceptionally if ever that any one kind of productive agency working alone can produce anything. "Land, labor and capital", and many kinds of some of them at least, must work together to create a product. That is, one kind of productive agency alone is not a productive agency at all, and the amount of product obtainable from any given amount of productive power in any particular form depends *altogether* on the proportions and the manner in which it is combined with productive power in other forms. In technical language, the demand for productive power is a joint demand for various forms of productive power. It is this fact which gives rise to a special problem of distribution, over and above the problem of the relation between price and cost of production. We know from the theory of normal price, and from observation of the plain facts of economic life, that the value of the product will be equal to the *combined* value of the productive services used in making it; but we have to have an explanation of the way in which that product value is divided among the different productive services, or the mechanism by which they are *separately* valued. The knowledge that if a bushel of wheat is worth two dollars the *joint* value of the use of certain quantities of land and various labor and capital services used in producing a bushel of wheat will be worth about two dollars, tells us nothing about the rent of an *acre* of land, the return of any kind of *machine* (or dollar invested in any kind of machinery) or the wages of a *day's work* of any kind of labor.

THE GENERAL PRINCIPLE UNDERLYING DISTRIBUTION OR THE "IMPUTATION" OF SHARES IN A PRODUCT TO PRODUCTIVE AGENCIES INDIVIDUALLY. VARIABILITY OF PROPORTIONS IN COMBINING PRODUCTIVE AGENCIES. DIMINISHING PHYSICAL RETURNS AND THE MARGINAL CONTRIBUTION OF EACH SERVICE. It has seemed to many students of the problem that its solution is a manifest impossibility. It would be merely absurd, it is said, to pretend that a batch of biscuit can

Distribution

be divided up into shares, so many produced by the cook, so many by the stove, etc., and just as absurd to say that of the yield of a wheat field so many bushels can be attributed to the land and so many to each of the other co-operating agencies of production. Looking at a single small organization, this may well seem to be the case. But the competitive system does make a division, of the product or of the money received for it, and it would seem to be the province of the economist to explain how it is done. A little reflection upon the well-known facts of productive relations will make the principle clear, and even simple.

It is true that the field alone would produce little if any wheat, and that the other agencies such as seed and labor could certainly produce none at all without the aid of some land. But it is also a matter of familiar knowledge that the proportions in which the other agencies are applied to the land are variable within rather wide limits, and that varying any one of them will affect the amount of the product. That is, although no wheat may be producible by any one agency or "factor", it is certain that *more* wheat can be produced by using *more* of one factor *without* using more of the others. That is, an *additional* acre of land alone or additional application or "dose" of labor or capital alone may, and ordinarily will, make an *addition* to the output. Furthermore, reasoning which is mathematical in character and is beyond the scope of a brief introductory treatment will show that if we take a large field with large amounts of labor and capital and consider the effect on the output of adding a *small* unit of land or labor or capital individually, we shall find that these additions to product do furnish a basis for distributing the whole product of the large organization among all the co-operating factors. That is, if we should ascertain the number of bushels of wheat added to the total output by a small addition of land to the large organization and multiply that addition to product by the number of such small units of land in the total organization, and do the same for the labor and capital, and add these products, we should in fact, under conditions similar to those which obtain in the actual conduct of industry, get a sum just equal to the total output of the organization. Hence it is very much more than a figure of speech to say that the land produces a certain share of the product, and similarly for each one of the other factors. If each unit of each factor is given a share in the output exactly equal to what any one unit of that factor adds to the total yield of all the factors working together, there will be just enough product to pay them all off on this basis.

Furthermore—and this is the important fact—the above reasoning is a true picture of the kind of calculation on the basis of which a business man does buy and use productive factors, in so far as he acts intelligently, in accord with scientific facts and economic motives. For surely it is clear that he does buy the productive factors individually and unit by unit, and that the decision whether or not to buy any particular unit of any particular factor depends precisely on the addition which that one unit will make to total output in relation to the addition it makes to total cost. This conception of the addition to the total output of an organization due to a small "increment" of a particular productive factor is the foundation of all distribution theory, because it is the foundation of the business man's policy in buying productive power and hence of the distribution process itself. It is generally called the "specific product" or "marginal product" of a productive service.

DEMAND, SUPPLY AND PRICE OF A PRODUCTIVE SERVICE. The argument just given shows how the demand for the use of one factor can be separated from the demand for factors jointly, how the value of one can be compared with the value of others. The relation between demand, supply and price is of the same pattern as in the case of any consumption good; particularly in that the relation between amount demanded and price is for any single purchaser the inverse of what it is for the market as a whole. For any single purchaser, the price determines the amount taken; in the market as a whole, there is a certain supply to be sold, and the competition of buyers and sellers sets a price that will clear the market, and neither more nor less.

This reasoning requires elaboration at one or two points in order to make it a satisfactory explanation of the pricing of productive services. In the first place, in view of the fact that demand is joint with the possibility of substitution, the demand for any productive service is strictly related to the demand for others. The purchaser of productive services is the producer in industry. His problem is two-fold: first, how much to buy of all productive services together; that is, how much of his particular commodity to produce; the second, how to apportion his expenditure among the different types of productive service, how much land, how much labor, how much capital and how much of various kinds of each, to use. The answers of producers to these two questions fix the two-fold apportionment of productive power referred to in our chapter on price, namely, the apportionment among commodities and the apportionment among enterprises in each industry. It will be simpler to consider first the problem of proportioning the factors, which is the more fundamental of the two.

From this point of view, the principle of the relation between demand, supply and price may be briefly stated. The proportions in which any entrepreneur will use the various factors depends upon their relative prices. The higher the price of labor, for instance, the less labor will be used and the more will capital or land be substituted for it. It is to be kept in mind that only the relative price of the different services is in question; it is taken for granted that all of them together will get the whole product, or in any particular case its total value; the amount of it that is to go to each factor separately is alone to be determined. For any single entrepreneur, the proportions of the factors depend on their relative prices, and the amount of all of them that he will buy depends on the cost of the most economical combination of factors in relation to the price of his product. But in society as a whole there is just a certain amount of each factor to be employed, or we shall assume for the moment that this is true. Under these conditions competition among buyers and sellers will set such prices that the existing supplies of all the services will be sold, that is, that they will be combined in the proportions in which they are available. Any single entrepreneur will buy additional units of any single productive service as long as the *addition* to his output made by it is worth more than the unit of service costs. The competition of the market tends to set prices which leave no residuum of any factor unemployed. That is, each productive service tends to be employed in the position where its "marginal productivity" is a maximum, and the price of each service tends to be equal to its marginal productivity under the condition that the total supply of all services is employed and employed in this most productive way.

Except for the complication due to joint demand, the principle is closely analogous to that of competitive price in relation to a consumption good. Price tends to equal marginal productivity in the one case as it tends to equal marginal utility in the other. The individual purchaser buys such an amount as to make the utility, or productivity, equal to the price and the competition of all purchasers as a group sets the price at the point at which the amount that purchasers will take will exhaust the total available supply. Productivity is in fact only indirect utility, as already explained; the productivity of a productive factor is the utility of its product, as measured by demand. The complication is that productivity has to be thought of as the *marginal contribution to the product* which is made by a *unit* of that productive service.

THE PRINCIPLE OF DIMINISHING PRODUCTIVITY FURTHER CONSIDERED. It will be evident that the above reasoning depends on the operation of a principle of diminishing utility and governs the entrepreneur's purchase of productive services in the same way that the principle of diminishing utility governs the consumer's purchases of commodities. That is, the producer apportions his expenditure for productive power among the different productive services in such a way that a dollar buys equal quantities of value-productivity in each form. It was explained in the discussion of normal price why productive power in general is subject to such a principle in connection with any one industry. This is a direct consequence of the principle of diminishing utility itself. As more and more units of any one product are turned out, that product falls in value, and of course the value of the productive power increasingly devoted to producing that product also falls. This is the more true when value is considered in relation to other commodities, for producing more of one product means (under given conditions of production at large) producing less of others, which other products tend to increase in value while the first decreases.

So much for the principle of diminishing productivity with respect to "productive-power-in-general". It also requires supplementing in being applied to any particular kind of productive power in relation to other kinds. When any one productive service, such as unskilled labor for example, is applied in increasing amounts to the production of some one commodity (being transferred from the production of others), in the first place the same thing happens as before. The output of the commodity produced by the industry into which the productive service is being transferred is increased, and the output of other commodities decreased, and the value of the first commodity in comparison with others falls off. But another change of equal importance takes place, operating in the same direction and intensifying the effect of the first. The technical efficacy of the transferred factor in increasing the *physical* output of the industry into which it is moved also decreases and its technical efficacy in increasing physical output in industries from which it is taken increases. If labor transferred from the production of corn to the production of wheat, without redistributing the other factors between the two industries, fewer bushels of wheat will be added to the total output by each laborer, and more bushels of corn will be subtracted from the total output of corn by each successive similar laborer transferred. This is in consequence of the decreasing amounts of other factors with which each unit of labor is being combined in the raising of wheat and the increasing proportion of other factors in the raising of corn.

Thus there are two principles of diminishing productivity, the physical law that successive equal applications of one factor to given amounts of other factors make decreasing additions to physical product, and the value law that the value of the additions made to product falls off still more rapidly. The two principles work together in determining the apportionment of factors among industries. It is of course the value of the product that interests the entrepreneur and determines the point at which he will stop adding further units of any factor in his business; it is values of marginal products which tend to be equalized for any factor in all industries in which it is used, by its apportionment among them, and it is the value of the marginal product which determines the payment for the service.

THE SUPPLY OF PRODUCTIVE SERVICES. The supply side of the price problem in connection with productive services is like the demand side in being analogous to the same problem in connection with consumption goods, but, as on the demand side, there are also special aspects of the situation. Questions similar to those dealt with in the preceding chapter arise in regard to the relation between supply and price in the short run and in the long run, and the answers are somewhat similar, but not exactly so.

It must be kept in mind that the problem of distribution is the problem of price in connection with productive *services*, the *use* of productive agencies, not the sale price of productive agencies themselves. This problem will be taken up in due time—for those productive agencies which can be bought and sold, that is for productive *property*. The agency which renders the most important productive service is the human being, and in our civilization only services of human beings can be bought and sold not the persons themselves. The sale value of a piece of property is in fact a fairly simple problem when the value of its use is known. It is found by capitalization, as observed above, in Chapter Three.

The first observation to be made about the supply of any productive service is that it is not necessarily fixed or independent of the price of the service, when the supply of the agent rendering the service is fixed. It is certainly true of productive *agencies*—laborers, natural agents and fundamental forms of capital as well as capital in the abstract—that their supply is practically fixed over considerable periods of time. But the amount of service which will be obtained from a given supply of laborers or productive property is not physically fixed, even at a moment, and may conceivably vary considerably as the price varies. The nature of this variation—the nature of the supply curve for productive service from given productive agencies—is a complicated question and cannot be dealt with in a brief analysis, but one or two principles may be briefly mentioned. In the first place, the variation of supply must be studied in relation to a permanent change in remuneration. The response to a price change expected to be temporary will naturally be different in character, and does not indicate the true connection between supply and price. When this precaution is taken, it will be found that, other things being equal, the relation is an inverse one; and *increase* in the *price* of a service will cause a *decrease* in the *supply,* and *vice versa.* An increase in wages will cause the same workers to do less work, if their wants remain unchanged. This is a simple application of the principle of diminishing utility and equalization at the margin; increased income enables them to afford more leisure as well as more of other commodities. If they behave rationally they will compromise between doing the same amount of work at a correspondingly greater money income and doing enough less work to earn the same income as before.

The second principle for emphasis is that theoretically the same conclusion holds for other factors than labor. An increase in the remuneration of land or capital enables the owner to use more of it for direct, non-industrial uses, in the same way that leisure represents the use of time and personal energy for non-industrial pursuits. In reality, other things are never equal, and it is impossible to predict on the basis of general principles what will happen. Experience indicates that the lower the grade of labor the more likely is an increase in wages to result in less work with approximately the same total in-

come for the worker. This holds typically for the employment of primitive peoples in the tropics—which is very
exasperating to the entrepreneur of European race and
traditions. Up to a certain point, higher wages will mean
more work, through better physical nourishment of the
worker, but there are narrow limits to this. Morale is a
more important consideration practically. With the
"higher" grades of personal service, and still more with
the other productive factors, an increase in remuneration
is likely to arouse new wants and ambitions which stimulates effort. Many brain workers love their work, or are so
interested in its results as to give to it practically all the
energy they are able to give. But even in our high-keyed
age and country, professional and office workers commonly work fewer hours in the day and year than laborers.

SUPPLY IN THE LONG-RUN. In the long run, we have the
question whether price affects the supply of the service by
affecting the supply of the factor rendering it. Here it is
necessary to consider the main types of factors separately;
we have in fact more than the three traditional groups to
distinguish, for there are important differences between
different kinds of classes of laborers, of natural agents
and of capital goods. Also, there are differences in the interpretation of the "long run"; and this problem subdi-
vides into a large number. In a very rough view, the
long-run supply of labor is a matter of the relation between wages and the growth of population; that of capital goods a matter of the relation between interest rate
and the saving and investment of capital, and that of
natural agents a matter of the relation between the
"rent" of such agents and the discovery and development
of new natural resources, together with its effect on the
rate of exhaustion of those already in use. Each of these
relations raises complicated problems, in regard to which
simple generalizations are of little value. In such a survey as this, all that can be attempted is an indication of
some of the questions which arise and a warning against
a few of the more serious fallacies into which the argument commonly falls.

Distribution

THE LONG-RUN SUPPLY OF "LAND". These fallacies are no-where better illustrated than in the case of "land" which term is used in economics to include all natural agencies as well as agricultural land. The traditional point of view in economic literature assumes that the supply of natural agencies is permanently fixed. That, indeed, is the proper significance of the term "natural"; the old definition of land included "the original and indestructible powers of the soil". It will be clear, however, that the really original and indestructible qualities are limited in number, and their value is inseparably bound up with the value of qualities which are the result of expenditure of labor and capital in the past. More careful investigation will raise doubt as to whether the total of what is called land value is in excess of the total expenditure upon natural re-sources in the past. It is largely if not altogether falla-cious to regard land as an unproduced good. The cost of exploration and development work, with accumulated interest on these costs, over and above all income taken out of the land, would *probably* account for all the land in the United States. There are few kinds of land which can-not be increased in supply even yet by making the neces-sary investment, whenever it is thought profitable, that is, when the necessary resources are expected to yield as much in that use as in competing uses. The main real difference between thus "producing" land and producing other forms of value is in the length of time one has to wait for a return and the high degree of uncertainty at-tending such operations, the large "aleatory" or gambling element involved in them. Some investments of this class do prove enormously profitable, sooner or later, while others become a partial or complete loss. The social prob-lem involved is therefore one of meeting management problems attended with a high degree of uncertainty and of variability in the return for a given outlay. The "single tax" argument that the increase in the value of land af-fords a peculiar "unearned increment" to landlords as a class, is without substantial foundation in the facts. The ethical issues involved in ownership of land apply in the same way to other forms of property, and also to many other cases in which individuals enjoy a superior eco-

nomic position based upon lucky commitments, long period accumulation, and inheritance.

THE LONG-RUN SUPPLY OF LABORERS.   In the long run, the
supply of laborers in a nation comes from two sources, immigration in relation to emigration, and birth-rates in relation to death-rates. In relation to immigration, the chief
popular fallacy rests upon failure to distinguish between
different classes of immigrants and the widely divergent
effects their coming has upon the different classes of the
population already in the country. Any immigrants who
do not bring property but only labor power into a country, tend to benefit property owners by increasing the supply of the other element in production and making the
property element relatively more significant. But this
does not mean that they injure all laborers. The immigration of unskilled laborers may in fact benefit the
skilled and educated classes of those who live by selling
their services as much as it benefits those whose income is
derived from land or capital investments.

Distinction between social classes is also necessary in
connection with the discussion of birth-rates and death-
rates in relation to wages and the supply of labor. The
effect of a given change in the wage-level may be very
different for different strata in the working population,
and it is always a complicated question how readily the
working population can shift from one occupation group
to another in response to a change in relative wages. In
the older discussion of these problems there was a tendency to lump the whole wage-earning population together. In a modern nation, certainly, this will not do at
all. Not only is there a great difference corresponding to
general social status, but there may be a nearly equal divergence between groups on approximately the same economic level, as for example between miners and factory
operatives or between either and railroad men or farm
hands.

Always the question of the effect of wages upon the
supply of labor must be discussed with a clear view of
the freedom to move into or out of the occupation group
in question as well as the habits and traditions of the

people who make the group itself. Careful students **no** longer speak in terms of a general "population problem" but relate their discussion carefully to time and place and conditions. The actual relation between income levels and the tendency of any defined population group to increase or decrease in numbers is too complex to enter upon at all in such a survey as this, and that is the important thing to be said about it. It will be evident that *if* and *insofar as*, any population group is isolated from other groups, and if and insofar as it has a "static standard of living", marrying and reproducing itself whenever its income is more than sufficient to maintain that fixed standard, and not marrying or not reproducing when its income is below that level, then in the long run its wages will tend toward the level which will just maintain the established standard of living. In fact, however, these "if's" are largely contrary to fact. Population groups are not isolated, and changes in income have as much effect in changing the level of expectations in the way of standards of living as they have in making people able or unable to marry, or have families, while maintaining a given standard. In many cases, certainly, a rise in wages will tend to decrease the birth-rate of a group rather than to increase it. And all such changes affect the supply of labor only after a period of from fifteen to twenty-five years, during which time many other things are certain to happen.

THE LONG-RUN SUPPLY OF CAPITAL GOODS. THE THEORY OF INTEREST AND OF SAVING.—INTEREST A MODE OF RECEIVING INCOME RATHER THAN A DISTINCT SHARE FROM A DISTINCT SOURCE. Undoubtedly the theory of interest is the most complex branch of distribution theory. The chief source of confusion in regard to it is failure to recognize the fact stated in the heading above, namely that interest is a special way of paying and receiving the income earned by any factor of production and not income earned or produced by a special productive factor. This is particularly true in connection with property income, but may be true even of wages. It is easiest to see in the case of income from land. It is surely a familar fact that the earnings of a piece of land may be regarded either as *rent* on the *land* or as *interest* on the *investment* in the land. It is less obvious in the case of other forms of property only because other property is not so commonly leased for a rental as is land. This, however, is *not* because other property is much less commonly exploited or utilized and managed by persons who do not really own it but pay the real owners for its use. A little scrutiny of this process of transferring property from an owner to a user who turns over to the owner the income which the property itself is expected to earn will help to clarify the nature of both interest and profit.

A farmer who wants the use of a piece of land which he cannot buy, or does not care to buy, may either lease it for a certain annual rental, which under competitive conditions will be approximately equal to the annual net product of the land, or he may "buy" the land, raising the money by borrowing. He may even borrow the "money" from the land owner himself, as not infrequently happens. In this case it is clear that the difference between paying interest and paying rent, or receiving the one and receiving the other, is purely a matter of form. Many considerations may operate to have the one form of agreement preferred to the other in a particular instance, but the chief one is the relative estimates of the owner and the operator of the future changes in value of the property. If the operator leases, he agrees to return the property as such at the termination of the lease; if he borrows money and buys, he agrees to return a certain amount of value. Other things being equal, a lease will naturally be used when the owner is more "optimistic" in regard to the property than the operator, and a sale when the operator is the optimist. The reason land is leased more commonly than most other forms of property is that provision can more easily be made to guarantee its return in its original condition, or some other condition specified and allowed for in the contract. The lease is also common enough in connection with buildings and many other forms of durable goods. But where the property is less durable, and in particular where it cannot be safeguarded against abuse which would seriously affect its value, leasing is impracticable, the transfer is mediated by sale and the payment takes the form of interest instead of rent.

THE INTEREST RATE AND THE SALE VALUE OF DURABLE GOODS. When durable goods are bought and sold, their value is determined by the operation called capitalization. That is, their value is simply the capital sum which, put at interest at the *current rate* will yield an income equal to the annual net product of the property sold. The product itself is determined by the distribution process already explained, and approximates the *addition* which a small unit of such property is capable of adding to the total product of a large combination of such property and the auxiliary productive factors, effectively organized and coordinated in production. In the process of capitalization, the interest rate is a *datum;* it "determines" the value of the productive agency capitalized, and is in no way affected by the purchase and sale of durable goods. To find how the interest rate itself is "determined" we have manifestly to look to transactions of some other kind.

THE CONTRAST BETWEEN A "STATIC" AND A "PROGRESSIVE" ECONOMIC SOCIETY IN RELATION TO INTEREST. The "other kind of transaction" in connection with which the interest rate is *made* instead of found is not far to seek. As everyone knows, money is not always borrowed for the purpose of *buying* productive property already in existence, but very commonly for the purpose of *constructing* or *creating* such property in one form or another. It would not be impossible to substitute a lease for the loan even in such a transaction, but it would be exceedingly inconvenient. The lender and the prospective operator would have to come to an agreement in regard to the construction, exploration, development or research to be undertaken, in all details, as well as to specify the condition in which it was to be turned back to the owner of the productive power going into it at the end of the period of the lease. Then, in most cases, the owner would look forward to coming into possession of a piece of property of whose use and value he would be ignorant. Manifestly, it is an infinitely better arrangement for the prospective operator to "lease" a certain quantity of command over productive power, take the responsibility for returning an equal sum, use the productive power in the way he knows how to use it to make it productive, and assume also the risk that the property he invests it in will be worth more or less than it cost when he is through using it.

In what is called a "static" society, that is, a society in which it were impossible to use productive power to create new durable productive goods, interest would be the mere equivalent of rent, as money would be borrowed and lent only for the *purchase* of goods. It is not certain that money would be borrowed and lent at all in such a society, that the leasing contract would not be exclusively used instead. If there were borrowing and lending, the rate of interest would be determined by forces altogether different from those which determine it in such a world as ours, where the predominating occasion for loans is the creation of productive wealth which did not previously exist.

In loans of this latter sort, the interest rate is not found but truly made—not, indeed to any great extent in any one such loan, but in the general competition of borrowers and lenders in connection with such loans as a class. The value of productive property of a freely reproducible sort is not determined by capitalization at an already existing interest rate, but by its *cost of production*, like other freely producible wealth. And the interest rate is "determined" by the relation between the value of the productive power necessary to construct a piece of productive property and the anticipated value of its product after it is made. Reflection upon the situation and motives of borrowers and lenders will show why this must be true— true, like other economic principles, insofar as the parties to the bargain know what they are doing and act in accord with economic motives. For it is evident that the amount per year which the borrower can be made to pay for the loan of a given sum is the amount of additional income he can count upon securing as a result of "investing" that sum, which is to say using it to create productive wealth. The lender, on his side, will secure as much as he can get, and the competition of other borrowers will generally force any particular borrower to pay about the full value of the loan.

Thus the same principles are at work as in the determination of any other price. The competition of borrowers in different fields of industry and within any one field tends to draw the loanable free productive power or liquid capital in society into the most productive forms of investment, and to force the borrowers to pay for its use according to its true productive value, as far as this can be known.

CAPITAL AND CAPITAL GOODS. SAVING AND INVESTMENT. DEMAND AND SUPPLY OF CAPITAL. THE INTEREST RATE. What is really loaned, then, in the only loans that affect the interest rate (in contrast with loans for the purchase of productive or other wealth, which do not affect it) is command over free productive power, or in effect, free productive power itself. This is *capital,* in contrast with concrete productive property, which is *capital goods.* The source of capital is *saving,* which is the production of more than one consumes. If one consumes his income, he directs productive power into the creation of the particular goods which he consumes. If he saves a part of it, and invests his savings, he directs productive power into the creation of productive wealth, in the same way, and instead of the satisfaction of consuming, the saver gets the ownership of the new capital goods, or a claim against their product which is ownership in effect, though the title may vest in someone else to whom he has loaned the saving. The real process of investment thus consists in the use of productive power, by the saver or someone who borrows his savings (directly or through a bank or other institution as an intermediary) to create new productive wealth (capital goods) *instead of* using it to create goods for immediate consumption. The significance of capital goods is, of course, to create, before they wear out, *more* consumption goods than were sacrificed in constructing them. If this could not be done, and if savers and investors in general did not know it could be done, interest could not be paid; and no saving and investment would take place, and little or no lending of "money", which is command over wealth in the abstract, in contrast with the leasing of concrete pieces of wealth. The current rate of interest therefore tends to represent the fraction or percentage of an investment which its embodiment in productive wealth will yield in one year over and above a sum sufficient to repay its cost during the period of its productive life.

So far, the explanation of interest has run in terms of demand. The demand for capital has been shown to be an indirect demand for capital goods, and the demand for capital goods is an indirect demand for their product —product meaning always net product or marginal contribution to production. The demand price is the rate which the borrower can afford to pay. But there is always a supply side of a price problem, the question of supply price as well as demand price. For the demand price depends upon the supply; the larger the supply the lower the price at which it will be taken out of the market. This law of demand holds good in the case of capital in the same way as with other goods. Capital also is subject to a *law of diminishing productivity,* though in a somewhat special sense, which needs a few words of explanation. Hitherto we have had occasion to discuss diminishing productivity chiefly with reference to a particular productive service in a particular use, as labor in producing wheat. We saw that as more labor is used in producing wheat, the value of a unit of labor for that use decreases (a) because the efficacy of labor in increasing the amount of wheat decreases as more labor is combined with a given amount of other factors and still further decreases (b) because the price of wheat falls as more is produced. Labor must be subject to diminishing productivity in industry as a whole for the first of these reasons. If there is an increase in the total supply of labor without an increase in the other factors, the labor will be at a disadvantage in its proportions to other factors in *every* industry. But because the increase in supply will tend to be distributed among all industries, the effect of a given increase in the total supply in reducing the marginal physical productivity will be relatively small.

The case of capital is similar, but in a more extreme degree. An increase in the supply of capital can flow into all industries, and in addition can take many different forms in each industry. Capital is therefore subject to diminishing returns to a lesser degree than any one productive factor in all industries (and of course to a still lesser degree as compared with any one factor in any one industry), because capital represents all the infinitely various productive factors which can be made by using it. In consequence, society can absorb a great deal of capital with a fairly small relative diminution in its productivity and its demand price; *the demand for capital is extremely elastic.*

The supply of capital comes, as already observed, from saving. The relation between the interest rate and saving is a matter of great uncertainty. Some persons would no doubt save more at a higher interest rate than at a lower one, while others would save less, and the effect on the total saving can only be guessed. There is, however, a fair presumption that the interest rate does not make a great deal of difference in the total rate of saving. And in any case, it is perfectly certain that the difference which would be made in six months of a year in the total supply of capital by the difference in saving which would result from any possible change in the interest rate would be very small in comparison to the supply already in the market. That is, *the supply of capital is extremely inelastic.* It follows that the demand side does dominate the price situation with regard to any moderate period of time; that is, the interest rate is determined by the marginal productivity of capital, and that marginal productivity is not greatly affected by supply considerations. The price of goods and services generally is the marginal demand price for the available supply, but in most cases the supply depends on the price in turn. However, with interest (the price of capital) this is not true.

The supply of capital comes from saving, and saving is often said to depend on the comparison which people generally make between present and future goods. The more they discount the future the less they will save, and vice versa. Hence it is argued that in the long run the interest rate depends on the general psychological disposition toward futurity or waiting. To some extent this is perhaps true. But the motives underlying saving are very complex and uncertain. One thing is obvious; the great bulk of the social supply of capital comes and must come from saving by persons who do not consume or expect to consume their saving at any time, but die and leave it behind them. It hardly seems real to refer to the motives for leaving an estate after death as a comparison between present and future goods. Other arguments still further weaken the view of psychological discounting as a main cause affecting the interest rate, but they cannot be given here. About all that can profitably be said about long-run tendencies is that capital is accumulating rapidly, which tends to bring down the interest rate, but inventions and discoveries are taking place and population is increasing, which tend to raise it by providing more productive uses for capital. Aside from the effects of wars, the rate shows a surprising steadiness and constancy in the course of history.

All discussion of "the" interest rate is necessarily abstract, and requires interpretation to relate it to the rate for a particular kind of loans at a particular place and time. The main factors causing divergence in the rate on different loans are the uncertainty of repayment, or "risk", and the trouble involved in making and renewing loans for small sums and over short periods. As between different parts of the world and different branches of industry, it is to be remarked that barriers impeding the flow of capital from points where it is abundant to places of scarcity do affect the rate very materially. The demand for capital in a limited section of a country or of the field of investment is by no means so elastic as that of a national or world market, and differences in supply become important. In advanced countries, in the short run, banking conditions and bank credit are a dominant factor in the supply of immediate funds for lending, but in the long run the bank affects the volume of circulating medium and the price level rather than the supply of capital.

RENT AND INTEREST IN RELATION TO THE DIFFERENT PRODUCTIVE FACTORS. It is common to think of rent as the return on natural agents, and of interest as the return on "capital". The foregoing explanation of interest shows why natural agents are somewhat more commonly leased for a rental than are artificial equipments goods, why it is more common to have the legal ownership of the latter type of productive wealth vested in the person directing its use, or especially in the person responsible for its existence in one form rather than another. It will also be clear, however, and indeed the fact cannot have escaped anyone's observation, that the income from nearly any form of concrete property, natural or artificial, may take either form. Even clothing—at least many kinds of clothing—may be rented, as well as railroad systems and patent rights. And money may be borrowed to purchase any kind of natural agent, in which case the interest is equivalent to a rent. Indeed, as already observed, the difference sometimes fades out more or less in relation to labor itself. One may borrow money to pay for an engineering or a medical education, which clearly gives the professional earnings the character of interest on investment.

Whether there is sufficient ground for regarding natural agents as a different productive factor from capital goods is a question too large to treat in detail here. Certainly the natural bases of economic life—climate, topography, mineral wealth and even soil fertility—stand in a different relation to public policy than that occupied by freely reproducible productive equipment. Yet in any particular instance, the intermixture of natural and artificial qualities, and of various conditions of reproducibility in the various qualities making a particular piece of wealth a source of income, seems to make any such dual classification misleading rather than helpful. Land and its manifold improvements form an indivisible unit. The more durable forms of capital goods approach the character of permanent natural resources in their relation to economic activity. Most features of land itself are either in effect producible at a cost or else are not really in themselves limiting factors in productive operations—like space and sunshine. Then too, the group of natural agents would certainly have to be split up into several sub-groups quite as distinct from each other as any of them would be from capital equipment. Pure situation value, such as land adjacent to a good harbor, soil fertility, and mineral deposits are utterly different as to the conditions under which the supply is maintained or increased. In short, as we have had to say in several connections, no simple generalization is useful. Salable sources of income have to be distinguished from many different standpoints and along many different lines, in accord with the requirements of different problems. The most important distinction is that between capital goods and land on the one hand (that is, any form of concrete productive wealth) and free capital (productive power not embodied in any concrete form) on the other.

THE THEORY OF PROFIT AND MONOPOLY GAIN. The nature of profit as a form of income now calls for a little further elaboration beyond the treatment already given (in the preceding chapter) in connection with the problem of normal price and its relation to cost of production. It was there explained that profit is a difference—positive in the case of "profit" and negative in the case of "loss"—between the income realized from the sale of a product and the total cost incurred in producing it, including in cost payment at the ordinary competitive rates for whatever personal service or use of his own property the producer himself puts into the productive operation, as well as his actual outlays for the services and property of other persons. Such differences arise because the process of distribution, or evaluating the productive services entering into a product, does not work with perfect accuracy. If this process did work with unfailing precision, the product value would be exactly distributed among the productive services, including those furnished by the owner of the business, and no profit or loss outside of payment for the owner's services would exist. The whole theory of normal price rests on this "tendency" of price and cost of production to be equal which is the negation of profit.

It was also explained that the reason for the inaccuracy of distribution and the occurrence of profit is essentially the inaccurate forecasting of demand by producers, and to a lesser degree the impossibility of predicting the physical result of a productive operation and so controlling it with precision. The latter cause applies especially to agriculture and industries affected by weather conditions. It is fairly apparent that if business men could foresee future conditions exactly, and if the relations between them were those of competition only, cost and price would always be equal, there would be no pure profit. We are concerned here with the first of these two phenomena, errors in estimating conditions and in making adjustments to them. The existence of conditions other than those of competition implies *monopoly gain,* a form of income often included under profit, but of a very different character from that now under discussion.

All that is here to be added to the discussion of the theory of profit is a few observations on the nature of risk and uncertainty or the reasons for inaccuracy in prediction. The first of these observations is that not all "risks" necessarily give rise to profit, or loss. Many kinds can be *insured against,* which eliminates them as factors of uncertainty. The principle of insurance is the application of the "law of large numbers", that in a large group of trials the proportion of occurrences to non-occurrences of a contingent event tends to be constant. The death of a particular individual, burning of a particular building, loss of a particular ship at sea, etc., is uncertain; but in a group of a hundred thousand similar cases the proportion of losses is very accurately predictable. There are many ways of applying this principle, in addition to the various forms of insurance called by the name. A large corporation, by broadening the scale of its operations, distributes and reduces its risks. Concentration of speculation in the hands of a professional class tends to make errors in judgment largely cancel out. The essential point for profit theory is that insofar as it is possible to insure by any method against risk, the cost of carrying it is converted into a constant element of expense, and it ceases to be a cause of profit and loss.

The uncertainties which persist as causes of profit are those which are uninsurable because there is no objective measure of the probability of gain or loss. This is true especially of the prediction of demand. It not only cannot be foreseen accurately, but there is no basis for saying that the probability of its being of one sort rather than another is of a certain value—as we can compute the chance that a man will live to a certain age. Situations in regard to which business judgment must be exercised do not repeat themselves with sufficient conformity to type to make possible a computation of probability.

It is further to be observed that a large part of the risks which give rise to profit are connected with progressive social change. Changes in demand and in methods of production, especially, cause large gains to some enterprises, and losses to others. And the work of exploring for and developing new natural resources is fraught with the greatest unpredictability, with corresponding frequency of large profits or losses. It is to be kept in mind that such changes do not merely "happen", giving rise to profit. The possibility of securing a profit in consequence of a change induces business men to make large expenditures in bringing about changes in every field. In the main, no doubt, changes thus induced are improvements, and represent real social progress. This is true of the discovery of natural resources and of more effective productive methods. It is not so certain in connection with the promotion of changes in wants. It was pointed out early in this book that the theory of individualism is especially weak at this point and that a large fraction of the political interference found necessary has to do with safeguarding the maintenance and improvement of society. Where distinctively human values are involved, the working of the profit motive is likely to give very unsatisfactory results.

The nature and source of *monopoly revenue* will be clear from the discussion of monopoly price. Where a producer can in any way prevent other persons from using productive resources in making a product equivalent to his own, or can bar them from using especially effective processes, he can make a gain by restricting output. It is to be observed that any individual rendering a unique personal service—such as an artist, or a professional man with a reputation causing his services to be in special demand—has a monopoly of a very distinctive and secure variety. As was pointed out in the last chapter, uniqueness is the very essence of monopoly. The greater part of advertising represents an effort to build up an impression of uniqueness, to establish what may be called a "psychological" uniqueness, in particular products, and thus to secure a degree of monopoly power.

Notes on Utility and Cost[1]

The general theory of equilibrium in a stationary economy of competitive free enterprise, formulated on the basis of a few simple and generally accepted assumptions, may be summed up in a few simple statements. Exchange value or price will measure at the same time the relative incremental utility of any two products and their relative cost. Cost may be measured in physical units of resource time, but the "real" cost of any product consists in or means the value of alternative products. The last part of the statement expressed the fact that resources are resources and not products, that their value significance is qualitatively and quantitatively that of products, actual or potential. The meaning of the cost principle is simply that resources are so apportioned among alternative uses as to yield equal product value all over the field. Cost is the reciprocal or obverse of productivity; equal cost of equal value is but another way of viewing equalized value productivity of resources.

The cost theory thus briefly summarized is in general that developed by the Austrians and Wicksteed, and the present writer has on various occasions attempted to give it clear and succinct formulation, and more or less to bring it into relation with other theories or modes of statement. The present paper may be regarded as a con-

[1] Published as two articles in German in the Zeitschrift für Nationaloekonomie (Vienna), Band VI, Heft 1, 3 (1935). In the published translation Sec. 13 and the last paragraph of Sec. 17 were deleted and have been here restored. A few minor revisions as compared with the translation have also been made.

tinuation and especially as a *correction* of a brief article in *The Journal of Political Economy* for June, 1928.[2] The former article sums up the general theory of cost in the following statement (italics of original dropped here) :

> The number of units of any commodity B which ex-
> changes in the market for one unit of any other com-
> modity A must be the number of units of B which are
> sacrificed in production in adding the last unit of A to
> the total produced (in the state of equilibrium; and
> noting that for units negligible in size 'next unit' may
> be substituted for 'last unit' . . .) (p. 359).

This statement assumes, and is obviously untrue unless the terms of choice between different uses of resources are such that at the margin resources, in transferring from one product to another, earn the same money income as before. That it is easy to think of cases in which resources are on a margin of indifference at different rates of remuneration and not at the same rate, does not prove that there may not for any pair of products be some resources marginal at the same money income. But it does suggest that this may not be true, and in any case it becomes important to analyze further the notion of the indifference margin.

In proceeding to examine the issues raised and to see what sort of cost theory can be held, and to what limitations it will be subject we will naturally begin by scrutinizing the simple and accepted assumptions underlying the doctrine as stated.

I

1. The discussion of cost must relate to an economic society in a form in which cost has a determinate quantitative meaning. The subject of discussion in economic theory involves two main sets of elements. The first is "economic behavior" on the part of individuals, the second the organization of individuals behaving economically, through the social mechanism known as free enterprise.

[2] Pages 353-370. Cf. also J.P.E., April 1931, pp. 210f., note 22.

Notes on Utility and Cost

2. Economic behavior, an idealized abstraction from actual behavior, which is more or less economic, is that of a choosing individual with (a) a given end of action the degree of achievement of which is known to himself, (b) given means of action, likewise measurable, and (c) confronted with alternative modes of using some or all of the given means to realize the end. The end is a known function of the quantities of means, of such form that the means used according to any mode are subject to diminishing effectiveness as larger quantities of any means are used in that way. That is, the system of technology is given and unchanging, in the inclusive sense, including "consumption" where any technique is involved (see below, Sec. 5). For simplicity, technical knowledge may be assumed to be entirely common, the "best" processes known in the society being available to and used by everyone. Under these conditions, the economic individual apportions his economic means among the alternative modes of use open, in such a way as to secure a maximum total effect; this is obviously achieved when the final small increment of means used according to each alternative mode in which any are used at all adds the same increment to the total result as an equivalent increment of the same means used according to every other mode.[3] The qualitatively homogeneous end of the individual's economic activity in terms of which comparisons are made is called utility or *want-satisfaction*.

3. A free enterprise organization is one in which the economic activity of a large number of individuals is organized through the medium of "productive units" each made up of one or more individuals and each of which, acting as a unit, buys the use of economic means in the competitive market from individuals in exchange for "money", and sells "products" in a competitive market,

[3] In mathematical terms the diffential rates of increase in the result with respect to amount of means applied are the same for all modes of use of any type of means.

to individuals, for money.[4] The economic means in the hands of an individual may include productive capacities of his own "person" and productive capacities in any other form of which he actually has disposal. In the present argument, it is assumed that the productive capacity of every individual is invariable; the individual neither parts with productive capacity through gift or exchange which alters his total, nor suffers loss through deterioration (under-maintenance), nor acquires it by any of the same or reciprocal operations. It may be noted expressly that personal capacities are in the same position as any other productive resources, apart from technical differences which must be specified. They are "property"—or property is an integral part of the owner's personality.

The two sets of markets involved—the market for productive services and the market for products—are assumed to be "perfect", in the sense that prices are always uniform, and the two are assumed to be perfectly coordinated, in the sense that the total money value expenditure of any enterprise for "productive services" (use of economic means) is always equal to the total money receipts for the "products" created by the use of such services. We also assume that "imputation" is both exhaustive and perfect; i.e., the payment for every increment of productive service is equal to the receipts for the increment of product dependent upon or added to the total by it. In such a system, products are simply services, bought at a certain time-rate by consumers. No "goods" are involved in purchase and sale, i.e., none of appreciable durability; social economic life is an organized mutuality in the rendering of services (production) for enjoyment (consumption). The concepts of wealth and capital have no place in the discussion.

4. In such an economic order the economic decisions and activities of any individual fall into two divisions or

[4] Money is to be thought of as "neutral" in the sense that it is of no significance in itself, but serves only as a means for achieving coincidence in exchange, and that all changes in its value and all activities, speculative or other, which tend to change the value of money, are abstracted.

stages, the administration of productive resources in securing money income, and the administration of money
income in procuring want-satisfaction.[5] *Prima facie,* both
sets of decisions involve the solution of an economic
problem, in the sense indicated above: incomes are made
to yield maximum utility by correct apportionment
among different commodities purchased, and productive
resources are made to yield maximum money income
(hence maximum utility) by correct apportionment
among different fields of production. *Prima facie,* the
two problem-solving activities are parallel, and on this
assumption rests the general theory of price as stated at
the outset.

II

5. Critical scrutiny of this two-fold administrative process shows first that the two sets of choices are not alike
or symmetrical with each other, and second that both
parts of the equilibrium theory (relative respectively to
utility and cost), are subject to serious theoretical limitations because they involve assumptions which diverge
from the typical facts of economic life. On the expenditure side, each individual has "given" a pure quantity of
a single, objective, homogeneous, fluid resource (money
income) which he utilizes entirely by apportioning it
among various lines of expenditure, in procuring "utility".
That is, he purchases different "products", and each unit
of each product represents an increment of utility.[6]

[5] Cf. below, esp. Secs. 13, 17, on the significance of the fact that
only part of the economic activity of individuals is organized
through the market.

[6] Utility is by definition simply the uniform abstractly quantitative aspect of products which leads consumers to purchase them.
But total utility is, within the range in which choice is made, a
decreasing function, presumably a different function for each
individual, of the quantity of each product purchased; otherwise only one product would be purchased, no choice would occur and no economic problem of consumption would exist.

Utility, and any product yielding utility, must be thought of
as a time-rate or intensity, not a thing. Even the notion of rate
is unfortunate, as it suggests a quantity spread over a period of

Notes on Utility and Cost

But there are three fundamental differences, or modes of asymmetry, between the economic problem of consumption—the use of money income to procure maximum utility—and that of production—the use of productive instruments to procure maximum money income.

FIRST: Productive capacity exists in the form of instruments of different kinds, in contrast with money income, which is of one kind. (In both cases, the use of the resource realizes a single homogeneous end, utility in the case of money income viewed as a resource, money income as end in the use of productive resources.) The organization of different kinds of resources in production is a technical problem and one of a different kind from any which arises in the subjective field of organizing final products in consumption.[7]

---

time. The dimensional relation is the inverse of this. The economic magnitude is inherently a process, something going on, not something existing. An anology such as that of hydraulics is misleading in that water exists whether it flows or not, and its rate of flow is a quantity divided by a time interval. The correct analogy for economics is current electricity, or better still, light, which cannot be thought of as existing without flowing. A quantity of light is inherently a two-dimensional concept, an intensity multiplied by a time, such as a candle-power-hour. The economic reality is of the same sort, a process going on in time. We cannot think of an instantaneous economic experience, still less plan for one. Economic life is a matter of the rendering and enjoyment of *service,* and economic society is basically an organized mutuality of services. (In the stationary society here considered, there is no exchange of capacity to render service, or property, and no increase or decrease in such capacity through "capital" production or its opposite—no under- or over-maintenance.) Different products—services of instruments, human or non-human—may be to any extent complementary in their utility yielding capacity.

[7] Consumption, in the sense of the objective division we are practically compelled to make between production and consumption, also presents technical problems. This separation is almost necessarily at the line of the spending *versus* making of

SECOND. The different kinds of productive instruments or resources are typically owned by different individuals, and *the productive capacity belonging to an individual* (especially labor power—productive capacity in other forms is in a more or less different situation to be discussed separately) is typically all put to a single mode of use. This is the principle of the division of labor; with division of labor absent, economic society or socialized economic life does not, generally speaking, arise at all, and with division of labor present, there is no apportioning by an individual of his personal earning power among different modes of income earning, corresponding to the allocation of spending power among consumable products.[8] The *social* organization of different kinds of productive capacity owned by different individuals is a

---

money income by the final consumer. Logically, production should *by definition* cover the entire technical or physical process, including even such activities as the buttering of bread and conveying of cooked and served food to the mouth, and even the physical act of eating in so far as it is conscious and purposive. Consumption is strictly the subjective enjoyment of products. But for practical purposes the economist is more interested in the social organization of economic life through market relations than in individual economic behavior as such, and this leads to inclusion in consumption of all that the final consumer does with products after they are permanently removed from the market. But the definiteness and permanence of separation of private economic activity from the market organization is a matter of degree. This fact is a source of profound difficulty in the study of the economic system. In particular it underlies the main difficulty which sets the central problem of the present discussion—the fact noted above that resources may receive a different remuneration on crossing an indifference line separating alternative occupations, the fact which upsets the cost theory of price in its simple form.

[8] In reality, of course, the division of labor in modern economic life is carried another stage beyond that involved in specialization on products; the creation of a single product in its labor aspect is regularly split up into a vast number of detailed operations assigned to different individuals, who often live on the other side of the world from one another.

different kind of process from the organization of the use of income by each individual separately.[9]

THIRD. The productive capacity owned by an individual is available for other uses than the procuring of money income—and is to a varying extent devoted to these other uses—while money income is not, in the nature of the case, available for any other use than the purchase of products. This qualification applies to productive capacity in most forms, external property as well as labor power. As a matter of fact, practically every form of productive capacity in the possession of every owner is by him apportioned in some way between these two general modes of use, while labor, at least, is not apportioned by any individual among a plurality of pecuniary uses. It is this competition of non-pecuniary employments for resources which gives rise to the notion of pain cost—which obviously exists in connection with other forms of productive capacity in the same sense as with labor. It is merely an aspect of the fact that the economic life of the individual is only partly organized into the social system of purchase and sale and management of technique by business units. But the division is not definite or fixed. On the contrary, there is *normally* a two-fold, shifting margin of indifference between the organized and the private economy. Most types of productive resources are more or less distributed between the two fields or modes of use, and at the same time most individual units of productive capacity are employed partly in both fields. This last applies especially to the human being himself, but largely to "property" also.[10] Theory must simply assume that

[9] Both products and productive services are typically complementary among themselves, while at the same time one kind or either may be substituted for another in some degree and with decreasing effectiveness; i.e., both products and productive services are always both complementary and competitive. But the meaning is utterly different in the two cases, as will be seen from the first and second principles of asymmetry.

[10] Because of the vague and shifting character of the division, it is impossible to adhere to the conception of the field for economic theory as bounded by the activities of the market system, or to

there is a boundary and that it coincides with the true logical division between production and consumption, including all production, and make corrections for the inaccuracy involved whenever it is sufficiently important for the issue being considered.

6.   In the money expenditure stage or phase of economic life, the economic principle of rational apportionment takes the form of the doctrine that in a perfect market at equilibrium, incremental utility measures or corresponds to price. The theory rests on two general principles or axioms; first, the principle of economic behavior, that

---

draw any clear boundaries. Personal self-service, and the use of "property" by the owner, may be only accidentally and formally outside the pecuniary system. That is, it may be a matter of indifference to the individual whether the given result is secured through personal self-service—or the use of his "own" property, as the case may be—or by earning the money through wages or leasing the property and buying in the market. Thus one may cook at home or work outside for money and hire it done or buy cooked food, and one may own one's own house or rent from another with the proceeds of some other investment of the "capital". Such an indifferent situation requires that the productive capacity used by the individual have a market value and that the service be procurable in the market, and that the resultant yield the same net utility as self-service. In most cases of self-service, the resultant is not the same, and the theoretical value equivalent of the self-service is moreover generally ambiguous, according as it is taken to be the sale value of the service capacity or the market cost of an equivalent service. The most important case which arises in the estimation of income is that of housework, though the total magnitude of self-service in the form of property—houses, furniture, means of conveyance, personal effects, etc.,—is very considerable. It is to be noted that the bulk of both personal and property service which does not go through the market is not strictly individual self-service, but involves a mutuality within some group, especially the members of a family. This leads to the general observation that all barter relations are technically outside of pecuniary economic society.

(This contrast between the pecuniary and non-pecuniary uses of resources will hardly be confused with that between pecuniary and industrial employment popularized by Veblen and Davenport.)

each individual apportions his money income among products in such a way as to get equal increments of utility for each smallest increment of expenditure for every product, and second, the market or arbitrage principle that there is only one price for the same product in a market. The major limitation upon the validity of the utility theory of price as a general principle is that it is not true that every individual buys and consumes every product, or is on an indifference margin with respect to doing so. It is of the essence of the doctrine of equalization as a social principle that no comparison is made between the utilities of different individuals. It is only the "relative", incremental utility which is equalized. More accurately, the price of the increments of different products having identical utility is the same. The relative price of any two products is properly a social, objective fact, but the incremental utility of a product (or increment of product having a given utility) is non-existent and meaningless for any individual who does not consume that product (or is not on an indifference margin with respect to it). The equalization principle is, then, generally valid only in a society where every individual buys and consumes every product, with differences only in the proportions (or is "on the margin" as to those not actually consumed). Incremental utility really measures price for any two products, for every individual consuming both (or on the margin).[11]

[11] It should be emphasized that the accurate form of the utility principle is the statement that *equal* price-increments of product correspond to *equal* utility increments. It is contrary to the principle of diminishing utility itself to say that the utilities of any other increments—ordinary physical units—are "proportional" to the price. This proposition negating proportionality holds for all subjective magnitudes. These are never really measured; the temperature of two objects, in the feeling sense, may be equal, but it is never possible to say that one is any numerical multiple of the other. Subjective magnitudes can never be compared quantitatively, but only ordinally, except at the equating point, and *a fortiori* can never be added or averaged.

Minor limitations of the utility principle can only be mentioned here. The notion of a utility increment presents difficulty,

Notes on Utility and Cost

Inquiry as to the conditions under which an individual will not actually consume any particular product, and so will not establish an indifference equivalence between it and others which he does consume, raises very complicated questions. To begin with, we may distinguish between two types of cases. In one type, he is "free" to do so, i.e., there is no physical or technical obstacle preventing it, but merely the fact of taste. This may again take the form that the individual has no desire at all for the product and would not consume it even if it were free and even if all other products were indefinitely high priced. Or, it may be that the individual has a potential disposition to consume but that at the existing price scale and with his given income the incremental utilities of final units of other products are higher than the initial utility of the one in question. The border line of this situation is, of course, the case in which one is on a margin without actual consumption.

The case of "unfreedom" is more interesting and important, but more difficult to discuss. The assumption underlying utility theory is that of literally "simultane-

---

because it seems to imply that total utility is real and is an increasing function of the quantity of any product, as long as that product is bought and consumed, and the idea of total utility is psychologically dubious. There are ways to get around the difficulty more or less satisfactorily, but this is not the place to go into the question of the ultimate nature of utility magnitudes, or the relation between the utility which has to be assumed in order to account for conduct on the lines of theoretical mechanics and people's actual feelings in deciding to buy products. There are, of course, limits to the divisibility of many lines of expenditure. In addition, there are reservations about accuracy of adjustment at the margin. For many items in an individual's budget, consumption will be carried to the point to which it would be carried if they cost nothing. This is partly a consequence of the disproportionate effort involved in making a small saving near the theoretical margin, and partly it is a principle of choice that none at all is frequently preferable to incomplete satisfaction in a particular line. But on the other hand it is often advisable on principle to stop before reaching the point of satiety, even where costs are inconsequential.

ous" consumption of all products in the budget. This condition is realized in practical effect if the individual can transfer his consumption from one product to another instantly and costlessly, or it is realized at equilibrium if the apportionment of his *time* among the different lines of consumption has been fully worked out, and if the final adjustment is independent of the direction in which the changes leading to it have taken place. That is, the adjustment must be assumed either to encounter no resistance, and so to take place instantly, or else to take place against a resistance of the nature of viscosity rather than of solid friction. It is, of course, the first assumption that is commonly made, consciously or unconsciously, i.e., that the consumer's expenditures conform instantly to the facts of his momentary utility surface. This does not mean that all products must literally be consumed simultaneously, but it means that transfers from one to another occur in both directions with relative frequency, and rather as a matter of routine, within the period for which the consumer's budget is made, and as the time spacing becomes more elongated, and transfers less regular, this assumption becomes more unrealistic. The budgeting of food items may be assumed to conform closely to the theory, but that of such items as travel is subject to a much wider margin of error, while the notion of rational allocation to an item which occurs but once in a lifetime can hardly be held to conform even approximately to economic rationality. If the matter is gone into at all carefully, it is apparent that the things one may do or may not do in the way of consuming "products" in large measure "go with" one's general mode of life. In particular, they largely go with one's place of residence and hence with one's occupation; different modes of expenditure of income present many interconnections and incompatibilities among themselves and also with the manner in which the income is secured. These considerations make the "elasticity of demand" a very complicated notion and in particular one which varies with the time interval allowed for change, as elasticity of supply is recognized as doing.

7. Turning to limitations on the principle of rational apportionment in connection with the use of productive resources in earning a money income, the main general observation is that the second and third of the three modes of asymmetry between this problem and that of using income to procure utility each constitutes an important *additional* limitation, in comparison with the expenditure side of the individual's economic life. This is particularly true of the second and third principles, as they affect labor-power. Insofar as there is effective division of labor, i.e., insofar as each individual laborer works at only one occupation, it is possible to speak of an equalization at equilibrium of money or money-value return to different units of labor only with respect to classes of laborers within each of which all individuals are qualitatively alike and all of whom transfer from one occupation to another within whatever range they transfer at all, without changing the *quantity* of labor furnished, as measured by the value of the added product and by income received. Only within the field of free transfer is equalization in question; if two laborers do not transfer on the same terms they do not represent the same relative quantities of labor when working in different industries, hence no definite relative quantities. The equalization principle can then at most apply to those laborers actually on an indifference margin between any two occupations at the position of equilibrium. But if any given laborer in transferring at an indifference margin from one occupation to another changes his total earnings there is no equalization of money-value returns to the same resource at equilibrium. Then we can argue in terms of equalization of returns to given productive capacity only if we either (a) take account of variations in the fraction of the laborer's assumed total capacity which is used to earn money income, or (b) include in income a varying amount of non-pecuniary product; and similarly for productive agencies other than labor insofar as the conditions hold. In such a case it will not be true that the quantities of the two products which have equal value at equilibrium will be the quantities either of which is subtracted from the total output in its industry to add the

other to total output in the other industry, and no simple conception of objective cost is applicable.

It is to be emphasized that the first mode of asymmetry, namely the fact that productive resources are of different kinds, which are employed in a relation of technical complementarity, does *not* call for any limitation or qualification of the equalization principle. Each type of resource is separately apportioned among whatever alternatives of use are open to it, in accord with the principle of maximizing total return by equalizing the *increment* of return resulting from the final increment of the resource in each alternative, in the same way whether it is used in combination with other resources or used alone. The questions affecting the character of equilibrium are then the two already noticed, homogeneity of units as affected by ownership by different individuals and equality of the amount of productive capacity used in different industries when an agency or unit is transferred from one to the other.

Limitation of the equalization principle in its application to productive resources, through restrictions on the freedom of the individual to transfer resources (here labor) from one use to another represents a difference in degree rather than one of kind as compared with the situation on the money expenditure side. Such limitation ties up closely with one aspect of the phenomenon of the division of labor. There are three fairly distinct grounds for the division of labor, namely innate and acquired individual differences, and technical convenience not dependent upon such differences. Insofar as individual specialization of occupation is based on natural differences in capacity or taste, the limitation on freedom to move is obviously of a categorical sort, though still a matter of degree. Specialization based on acquired differences of any sort involves freedom of movement only to the extent that the specialization itself is carried out rationally, on the basis of complete and correct foreknowledge of relevant future conditions. In other words, freedom obtains only before the specialization begins; afterwards, acquired differences are in the same case as natural. Specialization based on technical convenience is the only sort which leaves freedom unimpaired. Such specialization applies only to a very few general skills and to labor of the very lowest grade, and then only approximately. (But see later, Sec. 16, last note, on "the other side" of labor mobility.) Finally, it must be kept in mind that, as already noted, freedom of choice of occupation is largely relative to choice of one's mode of life on the consumption side. But a change of occupation is likely to involve a change in one's consumption budget more extensive than the change in occupation resulting from a readjustment of consumption as a starting point.

The principal topic of further inquiry, however, will have to do with the third source of asymmetry, i.e., the nature, causes, and consequences of the fact that transfers of productive capacity may involve a change in total money income, apart from cost of movement in a mechanical sense. Such transfers cannot be assumed to take place under the condition of "other things equal" as tested by the pecuniary measure. When a transfer involves a change in total pecuniary remuneration, it is no longer true that resources are so distributed as to receive equal remuneration *in money,* which is another way of saying that the theory of cost in the simple, *alternative-product* form breaks down. How much is left of the alternative cost principle as to validity, what it means, and what may be done to reformulate cost theory in a way to make it reasonably fit the facts of economic life is the main problem which remains to be considered. Preliminary to attacking this problem, however, it will be useful to glance briefly at the forms of cost theory as developed in the historical literature of economic thought.

III

8. The cost theory which has, in the main, been assumed in the classical tradition, and which in the development of that tradition has tended to become clarified and freed of admixture of other theories, is one of alternative product costs. But there are two versions of this type of theory confused in the literature, and the view as a whole is confused with a different type of cost doctrine. Moreover, the distinctions generally made, between entrepreneur's cost,

pain cost, real cost, resource cost, and the like, do not get at the underlying issues.

The labor-cost doctrine of the older writers involved the alternative-product reasoning in a fairly definite, if incomplete and confused, form. This is especially clear in Adam Smith's first, highly simplified, example of the deer and beaver, in *The Wealth of Nations*, Book I, Chapter vi. Smith's implicit reasoning runs in terms of labor, assumed to be allocated between occupations on grounds of technical convenience only as above suggested; i.e., a given laborer works either at deer or beaver production, not both. But he specifies "constant cost" of both commodities in terms of homogeneous, freely and frictionlessly transferable man-days. The real significance of this is a constant cost of either commodity in terms of the amount of the other given up to produce an additional unit of the first as its production expands. The basis of the argument is simply correct apportionment—equalization of the value of increments of yield. This principle, turned upside down, or viewed in reciprocal form, gives identical costs of equal values, or equal alternative values as reciprocally each the cost of the other, since it is the competing use and not the resource service itself which is the "real" cost. The reasoning also involves, "of course", though Smith perhaps did not realize it, a diminishing demand price for each commodity in terms of the other as relatively more of either comes to market. (Cost being uniform here for all units, the qualifier "marginal" or "incremental" though valid, is redundant.)

Labor in this account means the homogeneous productive service of human beings measured in units of individual's time. In effect it may stand for any physically measurable productive resource freely available for both lines of employment, and unreservedly used in one or the other. Pain, or "irksomeness", has in general no meaning unless it represents a variable alternative use of labor (resources) outside the field of production for sale. But the choice of varying degrees of working and not-working has no bearing on the case as long as its role is the same in alternative fields and to all resource units, and for the whole range of choice; i.e., as long as any unit of resource transferred from one industry to the other always maintains the same rate of production in money value terms.[12] Neither pain nor any form of psychological attitude toward either occupation really enters into Smith's reasoning. It holds exactly as well if we substitute, say, acreyears of land service for man-days of labor.[13] The theory will, in fact, be unaffected, even if there is a subjective difference between the two occupations, in the sense that an "hour's" work at one is preferable in any degree to an hour's work at the other, as long as workers (resource owners) choose to take or give the difference in the subjective cost of an "hour" at the respective occupations in the form of a compensating difference in the fractional number of hours worked—or to adjust their speed or manner of working in any other way—so as always to get the same total money income in both occupations. It is to be noted, however, that if we are to get Smith's result of a constant cost curve, we must assume all laborers alike, and must also assume complete division of labor. If laborers differ, or if the individual laborer combines the two occupations under the condition which obtains in combining lines of consumption, i.e., diminishing relative utility (increasing disutility) with changing proportions, the result will be increasing cost—of one product in terms of the other, which is the meaning of cost in the sense in which it "determines" price.

As already observed, when a number of productive agencies of different kinds cooperate in the production

[12] Economic theory has no proper concern with pain in any case; all alternatives must be assumed to offer different positive magnitudes of utility as long as life itself is chosen. Even if this were not so, and some choices were choices of lesser "disutility" rather than greater utility, the datum for economic analysis would be a preference-scale without distinction between positive and negative states.

[13] In fact, it still holds if there is no resource cost—say, if producers get the products by wishing, as long as they have to choose between one unit of one product and a fixed number of units of the other (and if there is some limit on the total amount of products to be had, so that they will command a price at all).

of particular products, the theory is not changed in principle, though strictly constant cost is rendered improbable. (Cost will *increase* more or less where output expands.) Each "factor" is apportioned independently, its proportion in combination with others in each use being variable, and reapportionment involves changes in proportions (except under the improbable condition that the conditions of mobility and of relative productivity in all uses are identical for all the factors). Increasing proportions of any "factor" in any use involve diminishing physical returns—and more rapidly decreasing value returns, but it is the physical relation which must be viewed as "determining" price. Decreasing physical returns from any relatively more mobile factor involves increasing cost of any product in terms of alternative products. The condition of production equilibrium is not affected by a plurality of factors cooperating in production.

Smith's next succeeding chapter after the deer-beaver discussion, i.e., Book I, Chapter vii, is perhaps the nearest approach to an exposition of these fundamentals to be met with for considerably over a century, or at least prior to Menger's *Grundsätze*, which is better in some respects, but inferior in others. The glaring defect in this chapter, and one which affects the work as a whole of all the classical writers, is the lack of understanding of the concepts of elementary analysis, though these had been fairly well worked out before Adam Smith was born. The economists did not understand the significance of increments of change (not to speak of the refinement of limiting ratios) in connection with the function of a single independent variable, and "still less" the principle of correlating an effect with an individual element in a causal complex by varying that element while holding the others constant. But in addition to failing to explain the quantitative relation between product price and the income of the factors individually, Smith leaves doubt in the reader's mind as to whether he really saw that his ordinary or average remuneration of a factor is simply the maximum equalized rate obtainable on an existing supply, without unemployment.

9. Smith, in his later chapters, did not hold up to the realistic relativism of Chapters vi and vii, and set a precedent for still wider departures from the straight course by Ricardo and his followers. The most important points for notice in a historical sketch would be the treatment of cost as pain instead of the use of resources (withdrawn from some *other* use, which is the "real" cost) and in connection with this the interpretation of the capital element as the sacrifice of abstinence and the shunting of land-use out of a cost-determining role. But the point for emphasis here is that to regard cost as pain instead of the (indivisible) use of productive agencies, including laborers, does not mean departure from the alternative-product principle, and that this principle gives the real position of the classical writers. Ricardo is as clear as it is possible to be (see *Principles,* Chapter iv) that the process of price fixation is one of equalizing the return on transferable resources through systematic transfer from less to more productive uses. And this, as we have seen, implies the alternative product conception of the final nature of cost. Senior is just as explicit (*Political Economy,* octavo edition, p. 97) as is also Cairnes (*Leading Principles,* p. 59). J. S. Mill is notably less explicit on the mechanism of adjustment, and is probably to be classed as holding, at least in his chapters on cost, the very different type of cost theory attributed below to Jevons.

The capital element in cost, like the labor element, was nominally accounted for as pain, but the real logic of the treatment of capital was rather that it merely supports labor in production instead of producing, and goes with labor, or labor goes with it, in fixed proportions in transfers between employments. Ricardo's labor cost theory is ostensibly a labor-and-capital theory (Cf. explicit statement, *Principles,* Gonner edition, p. 59), and is in substance as much a capital-cost as a labor cost theory; his alternative cost argument (Chapter iv) assumes that it is capital which moves from one field to another to secure equal return, carrying the corresponding labor with it.

Both Smith and Ricardo (as well as Mill) discussed differences in wages and profits in different occupations;

not differences in rent (Book I, Chapter xi), however, though in Smith's chapter on rent there are observations related to those he makes in Chapter x regarding the other two factor remunerations. Some of the differences are really "equalizing" while others relate to real differences in total long-run income. It goes without saying that no notice is taken of the difficulty which such differences raise for the equalizing principle and for cost theory, which is our special concern in this paper. It is interesting to note that Ricardo places more emphasis on sentimental preferences of the capitalist between employments for capital than on differences in the "irksomeness" of different occupations to the laborer. In Chapter i, Section II, also, his position on kinds of labor reduces to making the pay the measure of the work.

It is not clear whether land use was held by the classical writers to be outside of the cost relation because land was not supposed to be affected by "pain" or because land was considered to have only one use. There are traces of both views, both of which, of course, are entirely fallacious; the *owner* of land experiences "pain" in putting it to monetary instead of direct uses, which is the economic meaning of labor pain.

Land may be regarded as an extreme example of a relatively immobile resource, i.e., as one completely immobile, having only a single use. It has already been made clear that the cooperation of resources of different degrees of mobility affects neither the general principles of apportionment, nor value relations at equilibrium. But completely specialized resources present a difference from the standpoint of the relation of the service value to product price. From the side of "distribution", that is, the pricing of the specialized service itself, no difference results —assuming that the industry using a specialized resource is competitive. The "units" of the resource will be apportioned among enterprises in the same way, and each "unit" will get its incremental contribution to the product regardless of whether the competition for its use takes place between producers of a single product or of any number of different products. But the relation of the price of the service to product price may properly be said to be reversed; the payment to a specialized agency is "price-de-termined", while the payment to an agency competed for by different uses—or the use of the agency, itself—is "price-determining".

Thus the classical theory of rent as a residual share is valid in connection with productive agencies which actually are specialized, or insofar as they are. The question of actual classification of productive agencies into specialized and unspecialized cannot be taken up here, beyond noting that it would in no way correspond to the traditional "tri-partite" system of "land, labor, and capital"; it is almost wholly a matter of degree, and largely a matter of the length of time allowed for transfers from one field of use to another. It should hardly have taken a century and a half or so for economists to see that the "residual" idea is theoretically applicable to any instrument remuneration and that it is reducible to the product-increment principle; if all "other" instruments in a combination get their incremental contributions, and a particular one gets what is left, this last will also be getting its own incremental product. But the residual principle does have a certain special application to the case of "price-determined" remunerations.[14]

[14] Agriculture is perhaps at least as largely a stage in the production of manufactured products as it is a matter of producing different products, competing with manufacturers for the use of resources. The division between the operations carried on on the farm and those carried on elsewhere is a matter of shifting technological detail. But, again, the case is altered somewhat if we take the standpoint of a national economy largely concerned either in producing agricultural products in exchange for manufactures, or importing "raw produce" for a manufacturing industry, especially, again, if the latter is largely on an export basis.

This conception of agriculture as a separate industry gives a certain intelligibility to Mill's one-sided position regarding rent in the ninth proposition of his familar summary of value theory (*Principles*, Book III, Chapter xi). The statement that "when land capable of yielding rent in agriculture is applied to some other purpose, the rent which it would have yielded is an element in the cost of production of the commodity which it is employed to produce" without recognition of the converse case

Notes on Utility and Cost

The existence of agencies more specialized to particular uses and their employment in combination with those less specialized, is a sort of extreme case of the cooperation of agencies specialized (or mobile) in various degrees, and does not affect the validity of the principle of alternative-product cost.[15] This theory is valid for the determination of the relative price of any two products as long as any part of the productive capacity used in making one is also used in making the other, and is freely (continuously and costlessly) transferable between the two uses, under the *caeteris paribus* condition, especially as to unchanged total earnings. The chief limitations on these assumptions have to do with the two questions, first as to the possibility of treating two units of resource as homogeneous when they belong to different owners, and second as to the meaning of freedom of transfer when the conditions of choice between pecuniary and non-pecuniary employments are different in the two occupations.

The sacrifice cost of the classical writers, and which in greater or less degree still permeates the literature of economics (notably Marshall), is "really" alternative-product cost, so long, and insofar, as the real meaning is that of equalization of the pecuniary return on mobile resources through economic allocation between competing uses. It does not matter whether the rendering of service by resources in production is thought of as inherently or essentially "sacrifice", or as the brute fact of using given instruments, including the human being as a productive instrument for the production of a product having value,

---

may be defended from this standpoint. For the transfer of a little land from agriculture to industrial use would make land a free good in the latter field without noticeably affecting its value in the former, and conversely, the value of land for industrial purposes might be raised to famine levels by transferring into agriculture an amount of land negligible in that field. The immediate products of agriculture are, of course, numerous, and the final products into which they enter, innumerable, and this is largely true of any type or piece of land.

[15] Sometimes called displacement cost. Cf. Robbins, *Economic Journal*, March, 1934.

provided the issue or choice involved is that of using the same service or undergoing the same pain in making the product as in making another—"other things being equal". As a matter of fact, the principal resource used in production is even now the "labor" of human beings, and this was no doubt the case to a still greater extent, statistically speaking, a century or two ago. In this empirical, quantitative and partial sense, the labor cost theory can be defended. Moreover, productive property, in "land" or other forms, can be traced back historically to "abstinance", with allowance for miscalculation and imperfect foresight.

But the exposition of the theory that labor or pain is "the" cost of products, and the readiness of students and the reading public to accept it, has undoubtedly been associated with a completely different conception of cost and its relation to price, which is generally more or less mixed up with the alternative-equalization reasoning. This other doctrine is connected with the strange, primitive notion that labor is the "essence" of value in some metaphysical or absolute sense. Unless "labor" is defined in a question-begging way, this theory is almost entirely fallacious, but that the early writers more or less fully accepted it is clearly shown by the fact that Smith and the others started out from the necessity of labor as the basis of the existence of economic value.[16] The basic fallacy is

[16] Cf. Wieser, *Natural Value*, and Whitaker, *Labor Theory of Value in English Political Economy* on the three problems of value, its essence, measure, and cause.

This strange conception is unquestionably the basic fallacy in the main tradition of British classicism, one from which even Marshall was by no means free. Senior, of course, said as explicitly and emphatically as possible that labor cost has no significance in relation to price other than that of any other force limiting supply. This in itself is ambiguous, as the issue relates to two modes of limiting supply as will be brought out presently. Later on, as already noted, Senior came out explicitly for the equalization mechanism. Yet in the bulk of his argument, to say nothing of later writings of the school, it continued to be assumed that cost really means labor, or some form of pain. Senior's own main contribution to the system of classical dogma was, of course, the notion that the capital element in cost could

a confusion between absolute and relative value. If we could think of economic life with only one "product", with its value varying inversely with supply and supply limited by the competition of "leisure" uses for the time and energies of men and similar non-economic uses for other resources, it would make sense to say that labor was

---

be reduced to terms of pain in the form of abstinence and hence to homogeneity with labor cost. (He did *not* propose an abstinence theory of the rate of interest or profit; this view was read in to his work by Böhm-Bawerk who, however, gave a very different interpretation of J. S. Mill's identical theory.) The reasons for the tendency to assume that the economy of labor is in any sense different from the economy of any other factor limiting the supply of desirable (goods and) services present a psychological problem to the solution of which the present writer has at the moment no contribution to offer. (It may not be fanciful to suggest that the interconnected misconceptions of product, of cost, and of capital in the classical writers are tied up with the primitive theory of the origin of effort in the world as a punishment for sin: "In the sweat of thy face shalt thou eat bread". *Genesis*, 3, 19.) It should be obvious that labor or sacrifice has no quantitative character except as defined by an organized system of comparisons, and in fact none of a definite or real sort, apart from a developed social exchange system. As noted above, subjective factors have significance in economic analysis only to the extent that they change their roles with changes in the organization of production, i.e., as the "pain" changes in quantity when production shifts from one field to another, as measured by change in value product.

There is a labor-cost margin between any two products if the transfer of laborers (or of "labor") from one to the other without change in remuneration is an element in their relative supplies at different prices, just as there is a margin in terms of any "freely" transferable productive resource similarly involved. I cannot see, however, that there can ever be a *pain* cost margin in any proper sense, since pain is never in itself productive of economic value. There might conceivably be cases in which a separable element affecting relative supply would be the suffering of less pain in one occupation and more in another, so that it might be said that pain as such was transferred from one to the other. But under no imaginable conditions would the decrease and increase of pain occur to the same individuals, hence there would be no possibility of a quantitative comparison.

the basis and measure of value; but price, and the value which it measures, are purely a matter of relation between different products and are affected by cost only insofar as the latter influences their relative supplies. The nature of this influence it is the task of theory of cost and price to make clear.[17]

10. This "other" type of cost doctrine, diametrically opposed to the alternative product conception, is closely connected with the fact of specialized resources, and dis-

[17] Ricardo never really pretended to demonstrate a labor cost theory of value. In Chapter I of the *Political Economy*, he argues that value is approximately proportional to labor cost, but only on the ground that capital cost is also proportional to labor—which makes it logically just as much a capital cost theory—and also with the express assumption that quantity of labor is measured by the wage paid. In Chapters iv and xxx, as already noted, he makes it clear enough that he thinks of price as determined, through changes in relative supply, by the transfer of productive activity from one field to another, with an implied equilibrium conditioned by maximum return. His notion of the transfer of productive activity was that of a shift of labor-and-capital in unvarying proportions. (See explicit statement, Gonner edition, p. 59, that quantity of capital is the same thing as saying quantity of labor.) Smith sometimes implies clearly that the proportions of labor and capital are fixed (*Wealth of Nations*, Cannan edition, Vol. 1, pp. 419 at top, 422 at middle); but Chapter v of Book II is taken up with discussing the differences in the quantity of labor which equal capitals are capable of putting into motion, which "varies extremely according to the diversity of their employment". In this connection, Smith still assumes that the proportions are fixed in any given employment. Ricardo assumes in his work after Chapter I that he has demonstrated that value is rigorously determined by quantity of labor alone, no process of adjustment being indicated. Such reasoning is, in fact, characteristic in Ricardian price theory. It was this Ricardian pure assumption, which was taken over by Karl Marx, as the cornerstone of value theory in "scientific" socialism. Marx's own "demonstration" of the principle in the first pages of *Das Kapital* can hardly be taken as having been meant to be taken seriously. It is too obvious that the heterogeneity of use value, on the ground of which he dismisses that derivation of economic value, is fully as applicable to labor itself.

cussion of that topic naturally leads into it. Somewhat strange to say, it is found in a rather pure form, as contrasted with alternative-product theory, in the work of Jevons,[18] who was in so many respects one of the clearest and most profound analytical minds among the makers of the literature of economic theory. Jevons' theory of cost rests in the first place on the "classical" assumption that labor produces all value (which as already noted is still more than half true in statistical fact, though completely false and misleading as a principle). It then adds the assumption, almost entirely false, both empirically and in principle, and of which even Ricardo was not directly guilty, that labor is absolutely specialized, that each laborer is tied fast to the production of his particular product, unable to transfer on any terms to any other.[19] He assumes, in the third place, that labor is subject to "increasing disutility",[20] to the laborer, while his total product is subject to decreasing utility, to him. This latter is, of course, an entirely different matter from the decreasing relative utility of a particular product to a consumer with increasing *proportions* of that product to others in his consumption. It is also assumed (fourthly) that each laborer is free to work as much or as little as he chooses in return for the total product of his labor (less "deductions" for interest and rent); and (fifthly) that each exchanges his product for the products of other laborers in a perfect market. It is chiefly the second assump-

[18] *Theory of Political Economy*, Chapter iv, final section (pages 161-6, 4th edition), and Chapter v, *passim*.

[19] Jevons seems to assume in his discussion of capital that that factor, which in classical style increases the productivity of labor but does not itself produce, is competitively apportioned among different fields of use; but the roles played by capital and land or the payments for their use as costs in Jevons' theory do not affect the present argument and will not be further considered here.

[20] It is, of course, a much debated question whether the supply curve for labor as a function of its wage is ascending, horizontal, or descending. Mr. R. F. Harrod reaches the conclusion that it is descending (*Economic Journal*, Vol. 40, 1930, pp. 704-7) but his assumptions seem to me unwarranted, and the argument as a whole inconclusive. (Cf. below, Sec. 19.)

tion, that labor is specialized, which reverses the deer-and-beaver, constant resource-cost situation and which is important here. The first assumption, that "labor produces all wealth", need not cause confusion if one merely remembers to substitute in reading the more general "productive capacity" for "labor".

In such a productive organization as Jevons assumes, it is not justifiable to say that cost either "determines" or is equal to price in any general, social sense. The (marginal, incremental) utility of *every* product can be said to be "equal" at equilibrium for *each* consumer *of that product* to the (marginal, incremental) "disutility" (competing utility of leisure) of the productive capacity expended in producing the unit of the consumer's product, in his capacity of producer, which is exchanged for it. And, of course, the marginal utility of equally priced units of any two products will be equal to every consumer of both. But under these conditions there is no comparison of the "disutilities" (sacrificed non-pecuniary utilities) involved in the production of any two products, since no two products are ever produced by the same individual (and no individual works on an indifference margin between them); hence there is no possibility of saying anything about the relative costs of any two products, even at the equilibrium point—except, of course, in the sense of the market *value* of the productive services used to produce them. Under the conditions imposed, value cost is merely a reflection of the value of each product separately. Subjective costs do affect prices, for each product has a supply curve which is affected by the choices of every individual concerned in its production. But such costs are entirely incommensurable for different products and even for different units of the same product.[21]

[21] It is to be kept in mind that these limitations apply more or less on the side of expenditure—i.e., to the theory of utility and price—as well as on that of production, to the theory of price and cost. The psychology underlying the thinking embodied in the familiar slogan, "Equal pay for equal work", would make an interesting study. It is taken for granted that equal money remuneration means really equal pay, but the pecuniary defini-

11. What the later subjective value or Austrian school did in the field of cost was to revert to the simple view of production as a matter of allocating the entire capacity of any productive agency or factor-unit to the use most productive in money terms, thus equalizing pecuniary productivity for all units. This procedure, as noted above at the outset, ignores the possibility of a change in the earnings of any agency or unit in crossing an indifference margin from one field of use to another. In particular, it ignores "real" wage differences, differences not of the equalizing sort, and differences similar in principle in the yield of property in different fields of use.[22] These abstractions probably do not involve departure from reality very great in quantitative importance. But on the other hand it must be rather exceptional that the theory in this form exactly fits the facts and in particular cases the discrepancy will be wide. Both in the interest of completing the theory and for the sake of understanding the divergence of view between two great historical tendencies in economic thought, it is necessary to carry the analysis farther and explain as far as possible what is the meaning of cost where at equilibrium monetary returns to similar productive services (differently owned) are not equalized.

---

tion of the quantity of work is rejected. There is no doubt a difference in degree, but in principle, the two relations are alike; any general theory on the basis of which it is possible to call two monetary incomes equal, when the recipients do not expend them on exactly the same commodities, compels acceptance of the money measure as defining the quantity of service rendered in earning the income as well. In fact, even when the external physical expression or embodiment of income is identical, even as to proportional composition, the incomes of two individuals are equal as totals only on the assumption that the individuals are alike. As Jevons clearly stated (*Theory*, 4th edition, p. 14) but as the Austrian school failed to grasp, the utility principle rests on the relative utilities of components in consumption to identical individuals, and says nothing about the relative utility or "disutility" of anything to different individuals. All reference to the principle of diminishing utility in connection with income as a whole rests on social-moral premises entirely outside the field of economics as such.

[22] Cf. above, Sec. 4 and note.

PART TWO

Suggestions for the Reconstruction
of Cost Theory

IV

12. We turn now from criticism and history to a brief constructive summary of the theory of cost in its relation to supply and price. The starting point of all thinking in this field is the notion of "rational" choice, choice resulting in more rather than less of a desirable [1] result, hence in general of a maximum under given conditions. The problems of economic theory have to do, in the second place, with *continuing* alternatives, with the terms of choice between *streams or flows* of desirable result (see above, Sec. 5, note on dimensions) and all conditions affecting transfer from one alternative to another. The cost of any alternative (simple or complex) chosen is the alternative which has to be given up; where there is no alternative to a given experience, no choice, there is no economic problem, and cost has no meaning.[2]

[1] See above, Sec. 8.

[2] The scientific problems of explaining the phenomena from other standpoints,—physics, biology, psychology, history, etc.— would still exist. These other modes of explanation are always open in the case of what we call economic phenomena, but when explained or viewed from a causal standpoint in either the mechanical or the historical sense, the concept of economy has no meaning. Moreover, the concept of economy applies to motivated behavior only in so far as the motive is a definitely foreseen end of some sort; it does not apply, for instance, to explorative or problem-solving activity.

These distinctions define what seem to be the four or five

Notes on Utility and Cost

13. Speaking practically and in terms of the way in which men think in the time-space-matter world, the notion of economy involves the economy "of" something, or maximizing of yield from its use. What is economized, we call "means", or "resources" (the latter term seems to carry a somewhat more specific reference to economic means, or means as economized by rational choice and administration). More accurately, we economize the *use* of resources, use having always a time dimension. As already noted, this element of means or resources is not *logically* necessary; much of the theory of economics would hold in a situation where people lived by simply wishing, if we imagine appropriate conditions of choice attached to the wishes. But in the actual world, the "given conditions" under which we maximize yield or "utility" do result very largely from the limitation of fairly identifiable and even measurable means, including the capacities (we inaccurately say the "time" or even "time and energy") of the choosing individual in his immediate person and of external objects subject to his disposition and control.[3] In the nature of use capacity, or

---

main "approaches" to the phenomena of economic life as phenomena, and they apply to all human social processes or events. Such things can be viewed as: (a) natural phenomena, including animate nature; (b) motivated activity, with the motive a definite end (the ordinary point of view of economic theory); (c) activity motivated in ways more indefinite and obscure, including such "ends" as curiosity, novelty, problem-solving, value creation, and most of our social interests (which seem to be the real substance back of most of our economic wants); (d) culture-historical sequence. The last point of view detaches social phenomena rather completely from the world of nature, including that of human behavior in the literal sense. The clearest example is language, which is studied in terms of its own independent categories and laws, having much the same relation to human society as the science of botany has to the soil in which plants grow. Other human phenomena, including those of production, marketing, etc., can be studied in the same way.

[3] No clear boundaries can be set to the domain of action coming under the economic principle. The truth seems to be that all four of the viewpoints or approaches already distinguished are

economic capacity, will presently be found to reside the crux of the problem of cost. The type of analysis which economic theory gives is meaningful only if we can obtain a clear conception of a capacity or potentiality the yield of or on which is realizable in different ways or forms, among which the capacity is apportioned in accord with the economic principle of maximizing total yield through equalizing increments of return from equal increments of capacity in all the alternatives of use. (In mathematical terms, this will read, equalizing differential rates of increase in return in all the alternatives.)

Economic cost, then, consists in the renunciation of some "other" use of some resource or resource capacity in order to secure the benefit of the use to which it is actually devoted. The *uses* of resources alone may have direct or primary value. But the fact of comparison and choice among uses gives any resource capacity the value of the best use of the "last" unit, i.e., of *any* unit when the whole stock is employed in the best way. This may be zero, in which case the agency is a "free good" and as such is not a resource in the economic sense. Under competitive enterprise, as roughly defined at the outset of this paper, the capacity of any resource gets uniformly the *pecuniary* value of the incrementally most valuable "product", so that its employment in any less remunerative way involves a pecuniary loss. (All uses and values

---

elements or aspects of our activity rather than distinguishing marks of different kinds of activity. Economic activity is merely that in which the problem is predominantly economic, and the distinction must finally be more or less arbitrary. For example, the painting of a picture involves the use of resources, including especially the time and energies of the painter, as well as other material; it will hardly be contended that the problem is one of economizing these resources. Similarly, it is unrealistic to view a "social" occasion (in the sense indicated by the quotation marks, such as a conversation, a party, or a picnic) as an economic phenomenon. (A graduate class in economic theory will usually include a few individuals disposed to argue the question.) In such cases it is difficult to contend that there is any tendency for the human value realized to correspond with cost in a definable sense.

are to be thought of as having a time dimension, as "streams" or "intensities".)

It must be kept in mind that the conception of economy, of choice among resource-users, and of cost, does not necessarily involve different kinds of results from use. On the contrary, results must be quantitatively comparable, hence homogeneous in the quality of being valued. Alternatives of use are *modes* of using a resource in realizing a *given* result, and in an enterprise economy, the plurality of enterprises bidding for the use of a resource count as alternative modes of use open to its owner. There need be no other alternative open; these are enough, as already pointed out, to bring about imputation of the product value to the service. (Monopolistic action on the part of either owners or users is not in question here.)

14. The theoretical analysis of enterprise economy for the purpose of explaining cost-price relations will necessarily begin with extremely simplified conceptions, and will proceed by successive stages of complication toward the particular compromise between generality and applicability to the real conditions of economic life which appeals to the individual analyst as a stopping point.[4] Only a fairly complete discussion of the steps in such a development will enable one to be clear as to just what abstractions are involved at any stage; but only the briefest indication of the sequence can be given here. We start fiom the notion already developed of enterprise (in contrast with "exchange" economy) which is necessary to give rise to pecuniary cost and to distribution in any realistic sense. To secure any approach to realism, we must discuss the theory of enterprise under the condition of a complicated plurality of kinds of resources, distributed as to ownership in something like the manner characteristic of modern "free" society with its "property" system. Similarly, it is necessary to postulate certain technical and other conditions of organization: the production of each

[4] Cf. above, Sec. 12, on other points of view from which economic life may be studied.

individual "product", as named and priced in the market, is to be carried on by an indefinitely complex cooperation of different kinds of resources, each hired by enterprise on competitive terms, from diverse owners. And we must assume such technical conditions as will give rise to decreasing technical efficiency of the individual enterprise with increasing size, beyond fairly narrow limits, in order to have numerous enterprises in every "industry" and to have competition.[5]

Our problem has to do with the relation between cost and the selling price of products, especially with the question when and in what sense and how costs "determine" prices. It is assumed that prices at any time are determined by the supplies of goods and the tastes and pur-

[5] The question of the relation between size and efficiency in the individual firm is a very difficult one to discuss in general terms, as it depends largely on human and moral considerations and all sorts of subtle and accidental conditions. For perfect competition we must clearly have *either* complete specialization between firms—each firm making only one product and a large number making each, *or* similar conditions of joint production of given groups of products. It will not do in this connection to confuse firm with technical unit or plant as does Professor Pigou for example. (*Economics of Welfare,* Part II, Chapter xi, Section 6, 4th ed., pp. 219-26). There is little connection either way; a firm operates any number of plants and a given technical performance is divided up among a number of firms. The relation between size and efficiency in a plant is more of a mechanical problem and significant statements can be made in terms of general theory— (relations between length, surface, and volume—relation to human scale, increasing cost of coordination, etc.).

Nicholas Kaldor argues (*Economic Journal,* March, 1934) that the indivisibility of some element, finally the entrepreneurship or management factor, is the only explanation for the fact that size is not a matter of indifference in the efficiency of the firm. But management is typically in the hands of "boards" the members of which actually have innumerable other duties. Only under the condition of an individual manager restricted to that occupation exclusively (which is unusual and rarely or never prescribed) would this theory seem to be intelligible. In general, the notion of a quantity of management activity, if management is more than a routine, is difficult to visualize.

chasing power of consumers.[6] Costs then, influence prices only indirectly, as they influence the supply of products. Since price is relative, costs are chiefly significant through their effect on relative supply, though in view of differences inelasticity of demand absolute as well as relative supply must be taken into account. The cost which immediately affects supply and price is, under enterprise economy, the necessary money cost of the producing unit. The pecuniary costs of products are identical with the payments for productive services and with the incomes of product purchasers, so that variations in cost affect demand as well as supply. A complete account of costs and price must deal with the economic system as a whole, but in line with the usual practice we shall here consider only the effect of cost on supply, taking the consumer situation in its entirety as given. The problem of supply is that of the apportionment of resources, or resource capacity, which, as already pointed out, involves two phases, the apportionment among product-uses or "industries", in the earning of money income, and the apportionment between money earning and other uses. The latter is the fact underlying the notion of degree of utilization or a supply curve for the service of given factors of production.

The concepts with which any such abstract analysis must work involve movement toward a position of "equilibrium", at which under some given "fundamental conditions",[7] movement would cease. For such an equilib-

[6] Speculative accumulation is ignored; if products are thought of exclusively in their ultimate meaning of services, speculation is, of course, impossible.

[7] The fundamental conditions mean ultimately "given" individual members of the system, each individual being considered in three "aspects", (a) wants, (b) resources, and (c) technical knowledge. But, as already suggested, it is preferable to assume that the technical knowledge on the basis of which physical production is organized is common property in the society under discussion, so that any physical transformation will always be carried out in accordance with the most efficient technique available. Only in this way can the discussion abstract from technical detail and concern itself exclusively with the allocative or resource-apportionment aspect of economic organization.

rium to be unique, i.e., independent of the direction from which it is approached and of other accidents, it is necessary to assume that the resistance encountered in any movement of resources from one use to another is mechanically analogous to movement through a viscous medium. The speed of movement will then be proportional to the incentive to move, specifically to a price difference operating as a difference of pressure or "potential" on the analogy of mechanics.[8] But no matter how great the resistance in relation to the pressure, movement will always go on to the point of theoretical equilibrium, where the pressure difference is removed. (The resistance to movement—viscosity—would not have to be identical in opposite directions.) For the present analysis, we also abstract from anything analogous to inertia in the situation; movement will then, if conditions remain unchanged, stop at the equilibrium point and not go beyond it. This is important because if inertia carries any change beyond the point of theoretical equilibrium, the system is likely to go into oscillatory changes, more or less rapidly damped down, depending on the relation between inertia and the viscous friction encountered.[9]

[8] More accurately, the cause of movement is a difference between two pressure differences. The economic process must be thought of as a circuit flow of activity, in a vast complex of inter-connected circuits, each beginning with a human individual as a producer (owner of resources) and coming back to the same individual as consumer. Economic readjustment has the character of a transfer of this flow from one circuit or branch of a circuit to another. The creation of money income represents a stage at which all individuals are brought to a sort of equality of "potential".

At the level of the present analysis all payments for productive services are assumed to be "direct"; i.e., they are wages or "rents" in the sense of business usage; we abstract completely from the phenomenon of interest on loans as an alternative mode of payment for the use of property.

[9] The importance of the viscosity condition is that if there is friction of the sort which occurs between the surfaces of solids, the actual position of rest of a system released from any position other than that of equilibrium will only accidentally be at the equilibrium point, and may be at any distance at

These general conditions of readjustment should be thought of as applying to consumption as well as to production, i.e., to the transfer of money income from one field of expenditure to another as well as to the transfer of productive resources from one mode of income earning to another. In the present sketch, we shall also abstract from that aspect of friction which implies energy loss through heating effects, though the costs of economic movement create no very serious problem if the resistances behave on the analogy of viscosity.

15. To achieve any degree of realism, two sets of differences among resources as to mobility must be recognized (in addition to differences with respect to re-allocation between pecuniary and non-pecuniary use in connection with transfer from one pecuniary use to another). The first set consists of differences in the speed of re-apportionment, considered in relation to the pressure or price difference motivating the transfer, i.e., differences in the resistance to movement or viscosity. This difference may be continuous along a scale from very low to indefinitely high viscosity—from high to practically zero mobility. The more quickly mobile resources tend to come to equilibrium in relation to the existing allocation of the less mobile, at the same time that the latter move more slowly to their own position of equilibrium. Thus there is an infinite series of short-run and long-run equilibria,[10] the ultimate result being a complete equilibrium of the system, with reference to existing "fundamental conditions".

Differences of the second set relate to ultimate relative

---

either side of the latter, depending upon the starting point and the detailed facts of friction and inertia.

10 It seems unjustifiable to make a general dichotomy between "mobile" and "immobile" resources, and between short-run and long-run equilibrium or "normal" adjustment. It is all a matter of degree, as is the related distinction between "fixed" and "variable" expenses. Marshall's well known distinction between short-run and long-run normal price is thus condemned in principle; in detail, his theory involves numerous and serious confusions, which it would require a long essay to consider in detail.

adaptation or suitability of different resource types to different uses. These differences should not be oversimplified. It is unrealistic and unnecessary to treat productive resources in terms of any small number of "factors", each completely homogeneous and divisible into small units, and complementary in use with all the others. It would be much nearer the truth to consider all agency differences to be of the form of continuous gradation from one type into another, with the types or classes arbitrary. For convenience we may recognize classes separated by some degree of discontinuity, but also with a considerable range of variation in suitability within each class.

16. The major classes of productive agencies, or "factors of production" which should be recognized in general theory on the ground of unequalities affecting mobility can only be considered here in the most cursory way. In "free" society, i.e., where the labor capacity of every laborer must be "owned" by the individual laborer, it is clearly necessary to recognize a general distinction between labor and productive capacity embodied in instruments not subject to this restriction. At the level of abstraction to which the present study is restricted, where we do not consider any transfer of productive capacity of any kind which will change the total in the possession of any individual, or any other increase or decrease—any investment or disinvestment—the distinction is much less significant, but it is still necessary.

Under these conditions, an individual may still change the "form" in which productive capacity is embodied, provided he does not change the total in his possession,[11] and the possibilities of such changes in form are notably different as between the productive capacity of his own person and that of external property. Productive instruments of this external, non-human, sort have typically a limited service life, and to a greater or less extent partic-

[11] That is, does not invest or disinvest on net balance. But in the system here considered there are no capital values and productive capacity is merely a rate of producing net money return after provision for maintenance, hence a rate of perpetual return.

ular items admit of replacement by other items of different form in place of literal reduplication. With freedom of interchange of ownership, this freedom of replacement will not be restricted by the limited amount of property owned by a particular individual. The conditions which actually affect the freedom of physical transformation are a matter of infinite technical detail and cannot so much as be touched upon here. The significant point is that the possibility of replacement adds a new dimension or degree of freedom to mobility, which may be present to any extent from zero to infinity, along with the various degrees of speed and cost of transfer, in a concrete instrument.

As regards personal or labor capacity, mobility is in the first place restricted by the indivisibility of the human unit, the principle of the division of labor. Secondly, the opportunity of transformation takes the form of restraining only, and this also affects the individual as a unit, and in general is much more restricted than in the case of non-human instruments. The replacement of an entire individual (laborer) by one of a different type is not, in free society, carried out on the basis of economic calculations, hence not in accord with economic principles, and so cannot be considered in individualistic economic theory.[12] The third generic difference in the conditions

[12] Many features of the working of family, group, and social interests and policies operate to adapt individual productive capacities more or less to demand conditions from generation to generation, but not to an extent justifying the treatment of the phenomena according to economic principles. Economic theory must apparently begin with the individual as a free contracting member of the market organization, and the changes he can make in himself subsequently are restricted indeed.

The transformation is generally carried out at a cost in either case, and here again there is an important difference between the laborer and property items. In a continuing economic society, the latter must be assumed to have been created in the first place with the transformation in view, and consequently the cost of the change is "written off" out of the net yield of the item during its service life. The laborer cannot be assumed to have resulted from rational investment, and a similar cal-

affecting mobility is the inseparability in space and time of the laborer as owner from the laborer as productive instrument, while at his work. This fact gives enormously greater significance to subjective preference between occupations on other grounds than pecuniary remuneration, and hence to the phenomenon of re-apportionment between pecuniary and non-pecuniary use in connection with transfers.[13]

All the limitations of the alternative-product cost principle arise especially in connection with the labor element in cost, and the further discussion may well relate directly to the labor element. The qualifications needed to take account of peculiar features of property elements in cost will not involve serious difficulties.[14]

The bare fact that there are differences in wages and rates of return on capital or concrete property, some of

---

culation is applicable only to the extent that he can actually retrain himself without a sacrifice of earning capacity. In his case, there is no possibility of an objective separation of that element in his mobility which results from retraining, from other elements.

[13] Such preference is by no means absent in the case of property, as was noticed by both Smith and Ricardo. But even where the individual has a strong sentimental repugnance to a particular use of property, he is generally not averse to exchanging with some other individual, so that the mobility of property between employments is much less affected by the preferences of individual owners; it is only where the preference is practically universal in a population, or where a particular use is prohibited by law, or the like, that these sentiments find much expression in differences in remuneration.

[14] The general topic of labor mobility cannot be taken up here, but one point should be at least mentioned somewhere in the argument, because it is important and commonly overlooked. It is that the laborer is variously and often strongly affected by a preference for stability or movement, "as such". This applies to property also on the side of fixity, though probably to a lesser degree even there, but hardly at all on that of mobility. In connection with labor, the "reluctance" to change occupations is much harped upon, but the tendency to change, for the sake of change, which is perhaps fully as important in reality, is generally overlooked.

which persist in the fact of freedom of choice, is an economic commonplace. Economists from Smith to Marshall have recognized that different occupations present different bundles of "advantages" and "disadvantages" and that choice is made on the basis of the "net advantages" of occupations. But such statements cloak problems the answers to which are obscure. For to the extent either that similar laborers get different wages or that laborers are different, it is impossible to speak of equalization of reward to sacrifice, or return to outlay in utility terms. The classical writers have never reconciled their cost theory with utility principles at this point, and the "Austrians" have failed to recognize the difficulty at all. They failed to see the categorical difference between the individual allocation of income and the social allocation of productive capacity.

17. SUMMARIZING: The apparent discontinuity in the terms of choice between occupations, arises out of three basic facts. The first is that the labor capacity of any laborer is apportioned between pecuniary and non-pecuniary uses. Secondly, in consequence of the division of labor, the labor capacity of a particular laborer is *not* apportioned among different pecuniary uses, but that portion of it which is used at all in earning money income is typically devoted to some single occupation. Thirdly, the terms of choice between pecuniary and non-pecuniary utilities vary from one pecuniary occupation to another.[15]

[15] The apportionment of capacity between pecuniary and non-pecuniary uses is an aspect of the problem of the boundaries of the pecuniary organization already mentioned. This dividing line is vague in two respects, or along two dimensions. In the first place, it may be a matter of indifference whether a particular instrumentality is used through the medium of pecuniary relations or in the direct satisfaction of the wants of its owner. And when a particular agency is used partly in one field and partly in the other, the vagueness of the boundary is still more pronounced. Yet we clearly have to recognize such divisions in mode of use of individual resource-items in economic analysis. It is common enough for the laborer, in ad-

Notes on Utility and Cost

If the principles of economic theory are to be applied to the organization of production, it must be possible to discover in it a process of equalizing the return on given productive capacity by an appropriate apportionment among alternative modes of use. But it must be clear that under division of labor there is no equalization of return from resources allocated among different productive uses in the sense in which there is equalization of return ("utility") from different uses of income in consumption. In the field of expenditure, we can say that at equilibrium all dollars or cents buy equal utilities in the relative sense, regardless of who spends them (in so far as all consumers buy all products). The allocation in production of resources variously owned, with equalization of return, is a process carried out by the social organization as a whole and not by each individual apportioning his own resources. The diminishing effectiveness of additional applications of a given productive resource in a given employment is an utterly different matter from that met with in the application of increasing amounts of income by an individual to the purchase of a given product. The former process is not one of proportioning subjective effects of a given objective agency, the effects being compared in a given sensorium and independently

---

dition to a money earning occupation, to pursue other employment, the result of which has a more or less definite pecuniary value, and cannot be excluded from the socially organized and measured economic activity. (Cf. above, Sec. 4.) Similarly as to property; a house or an automobile may be used partly to bring a money return and partly for "consumption" purposes, and the consumption, as well as the production, use may be such as would be bought in the market if it were not thus directly provided. The vagueness of the apportionment is aggravated when the value of an item such as a car in both the pecuniary and non-pecuniary field is largely that of availability for use rather than actual full-capacity use.

While this paper is being revised, Professor Robbins, referring to Viner, throws out the suggestion (*Economic Journal*, January, 1934) that the difficulty can be taken care of under the theory of joint products. The further analysis will show that the situation is more complex than this suggestion assumes.

for each individual; the units of resources are affected with the subjective interests of various owners and the effects are compared and measured in different sensoria. Consequently, if there is any effective equalization, it must run in objective or absolute terms—unless we are to be involved in comparing the utility magnitudes of different individuals, the negative of which is the fundamental principle of the equalization of returns in expenditure.[16] Thus in fundamental respects the allocation problem on the side of resources is antithetical to that on the side of income expenditure.

18. In the field of production, we can say that at equilibrium similar units of productive capacity earn equal incomes only if both the productive capacity itself and the income earned can be defined and measured in purely objective terms. The effects of differences in the subjective attitudes of different owners must be inoperative, and productive organization reduced to a matter of making physical resources produce a maximum money return, uninfluenced by other considerations. The cost principle will apply, or relative cost can be said to determine the relative values of two products, if and only if at any equilibrium point the relative supply of the two is determined at a margin of indifference by resources which will move from one field to the other in response to the least difference in pecuniary value of product.

[16] The business enterprise allocates its productive expenditure by varying proportions among a wide variety of fields, but this is not true of the ultimate owner of productive resources; the division of labor excludes such allocation of that resource, and unless the individual's ownership of any form of property or of "capital" is very large, there is no occasion on grounds of efficiency for distributing its use; if this is done it is on grounds of reducing risk.

In a Crusoe economy, all this would be different. A Crusoe would, of course, apportion individually all the resources used in his economy. He would not presumably, however, separate his management problem into the two parts of earning a maximum income in exchange value and converting it into a maximum income in utility.

Notes on Utility and Cost

In relation to the difficulties already explained, this situation requires either (a) that the entire earning capacity of the agencies in question be devoted exclusively to money earning, *or* (b) that a fixed fraction of their capacity be so devoted, as attested by equality of earnings in case of transfer. If there is a division between pecuniary and other uses, this second alternative means either that there is no freedom of varying the apportionment or no incentive to do so, when the capacity-fraction used for money earning is transferred from one money-earning use to another. Obviously, this condition may hold at the margin for some portions of the curve and not for others, during an extensive shift of pecuniary production from one field to another. It will hold at all points on the curve if all resources which are ever transferred obey the principle stated. But different resource units may not be indifferent at the same price point. They may differ in two ways, either in relative physical suitability for the different uses (as already noted) or/and in what we may call subjective suitability, due to difference in the preference of the respective owners between the fields. Then if production is shifted from one field to another in consequence of a shift in relative yield, units will move successively in an order determined by the resultant of physical and subjective suitability.

When the economic system is in equilibrium at a particular price point, all resource units not actually on a margin of indifference must be said to receive "rent" in the proper theoretical sense, and their remunerations do not "enter into" price. Under these conditions, it is not true that every unit of a product is marginal; only the units produced in part by resources actually on a margin of indifference at the same level of pecuniary remuneration are marginal units of product. It is not true, either, that all units of a given product have the same cost; they do not, unless all the resources used in producing the total output are either on a margin of indifference under existing conditions, including existing total income, or else have no other use and receive a pure rent, not included in the cost. Where these conditions do not obtain, it is not permissible to speak of "the" cost of a product, but only of the cost of some particular unit, with regard to all the special circumstances of its production. In a competitive market all units of a homogeneous product will bear the same price, and if production is carried on under conditions of effective competition between enterprises, all units will have the same money cost, regardless of similarity or dissimilarity, physical or subjective, in resources used to produce them. But there is no relation on the production side between product units, whether similar or dissimilar, and no comparability as to their costs, except through free transferability of resources and displacement of one product unit by another in production. And all money costs of a product, other than remuneration for freely transferable resources, are derivative from the price of that product alone. Yet if the product competes with non-pecuniary uses of any resources, the remuneration will constitute, or more accurately, will reflect and measure, a price determined cost, in the absolute, or what we are calling the Jevonian sense.[17]

[17] There is a further consideration which seriously complicates a cost theory on Jevonian lines, in addition to the fact that it involves no cost comparison between different products. Every supply curve corresponding to such costs is not merely an absolute, but is made up of as many absolute supply curves as there are resource-owners engaged or potentially engaged in producing the product in question. Cf. also below.

Still further, it is an awkward consideration that the effect of product price on supply in such a case might in the abstract be either positive or negative, and under the most reasonable simple assumption as to the character of the utility surface involved, it is zero. If we assume that the total utility of "leisure" (the alternative to doing *more* work at *any* margin) and of money income is a product of two expressions, each giving utility as proportional to quantity with any exponent $[U_{ab} = A^r B^s]$ then the ordinary test for a maximum shows at once that the amount of leisure a person will give up in exchange for income is independent of the ratio of exchange between the two. The multiplication of functions is the simplest way of indicating the complementary relation which certainly exist between income and leisure; any other functions expressing complementarity will yield approximately the same result.

Notes on Utility and Cost

Resources may be imperfectly transferable in all degrees between different enterprises producing the same product, as well as between those producing different products and between any money-earning occupation and other uses. Each of these modes of immobility may be regarded as giving rise to a corresponding species of rent. The "Ricardian" conception of rent really implied "infinite" immobility between a particular money earning use and any other use, pecuniary or non-pecuniary, i.e., complete specialization. It was interpreted still more confusedly as use in pecuniary production without "pain" (really, with no non-pecuniary competition) of an agency which itself had historically come into existence without pain cost or cost of any other kind. Of course there are no such agencies, outside of purely chance "finds", and there is every reason to believe that accidental excess of value over cost in instances where it occurs is enormously overbalanced by differences in the opposite direction. (The phenomenon of negative profit in explorative and promotional activity cannot be taken up here.)

19. If we are to be able to say that the relative cost of two different products determines their relative price, *every unit* of each must be *in part* produced by resources on a margin of indifference between the two at the same money income. Nothing can be said about the relative cost of any units of which this is not true. The resource(s) which is (are) fluid need not be the same physically or as to ownership for different units of either product, but the owner of any fluid resource unit must be indifferent between the two uses in all regards except money earnings. Where resources are on a margin of indifference at different money incomes, we have a mixture of the true price-determining cost principle with cost in the Jevonian sense above discussed, and any admixture of this element makes it impossible to speak of the relative cost of products determined price (price being inherently a relation). If the transfer of an agency from one occupation to another involves a change in money remuneration, it must be considered that at the same time its productive capacity has been reapportioned between the

money-earning and direct utility fields, an increase in remuneration representing a transfer of a corresponding amount of capacity from the latter field to money-earning and *vice versa*.

20. It is difficult to formulate conditions under which the laborer choosing rationally can be counted upon to be indifferent between two occupations on condition of earning the same money income in both; that is, it is difficult to do much more than to give a truistical description of the situation in terms of this result itself, as "such that" the situation will obtain. In choosing his occupation, the worker confronts a situation involving three sets of factors. These are, first, the money income, meaning the utilities which will be bought with the money; second, the actual work done to earn the money; and third, the non-pecuniary utilities alternative to the work and given up in working. Of course it is not generally true that the laborer can choose between working and not working, on the whole, but most lines of work present an opportunity to vary in some degree, and usually in diverse ways, the proportions between working and other uses of one's powers. In choosing rationally between the occupations, the worker must be supposed to compare them with respect to a net utility which is the difference between the utility of the (products to be purchased with the) wage on the one hand and on the other another difference, the loss in utility involved in performing the work in question instead of using one's powers in the most desirable alternative way open.

There is no presumption that any one of the three elements in the choice will be the same in two occupations. In the first place, it will rarely happen that the money earned by working at two different occupations will be spent for exactly the same quantities of the same list of products.[18] The opportunities for expenditure will

[18] This difficulty suggests one still deeper and theoretically more serious, namely that it is rarely possible to tell exactly what the *net* money wage of an occupation is. A part of the nominal wage will usually be spent for items which are properly expenses connected with the work—tools, special clothing, transportation and

be more or less different according as one works at one occupation or the other, and one's tastes, especially those affected by recreative needs, will perhaps be still more affected.

That the work performed in two occupations will be different in literally countless ways bearing psychological effects, goes without saying.

And it is surely apparent, also, that the alternatives to work, at the margin, will ordinarily be significantly different in the opportunities they present to create utility. It is to be kept in mind that the alternatives "at the margin", i.e., those which can be combined with a given occupation, are a different matter from the worker's abstract preferences as to the mode of using his personal resources. His calculations will also be strongly affected by the complementary relation already referred to between income itself and opportunity for non-money-earning activity (including in activity all willed experience); in large degree such activity calls for money spending. Moreover, the character of the non-work activities available is affected by the money-spending opportunities open, which are likely to be significantly different according to the occupation pursued, especially where difference in locality is involved.

Insofar as the alternatives which are the variables in choice are different, no knowledge of the choosing individual's utility surface as it determines the apportionment of capacity in one case will make it possible to predict what apportionment would be made in the other. Consequently, there is no assurance that the condition of indifference between the two occupations would involve equality of money income, even if the worker had

the like, not to go into social obligations and pressures upon one's living standards. Such outlays are deductions from wages rather than true consumption expenditures, yet most of them will have utility elements—they will replace more or less effectively expenditures which would be made in the absence of constraint. In general, it would be impossible for the worker himself to place any definite money value on these restrictions, or separate the deductions from wages, from pure purchase of consumption utility.

complete freedom to vary the proportional distribution of his work capacity between work and other fields of use. Generally speaking, the worker has relatively little freedom in this regard. Where work is organized on a group basis, there is a strong pressure toward standard-izing both the hours and the speed of work. And where work involves cooperation between the laborer and a heavy fixed investment, there is a further pressure toward maximizing the total performance of the organization and hence of every element in it. (This can be reduced somewhat as to hours, though not as to speed, by ar-rangements for working in shifts and provision of sub-stitute workers.)

Even if all these four conditions happen to be such that the terms of indifference between occupations in-volve equality of money income for all workers at all points on the scale, it still cannot be said that any two product units, whether of different products or the same product, have equal subjective costs unless the total as well as the marginal utility functions of all workers are identical. Thus there is a relatively complete failure of parallelism between the equalization of utility in ex-penditure and the equalization of return from a given sacrifice in production. In short, where there is division of labor there can hardly be any meaning in the notion of subjective cost as a determinant of price over any considerable area of the field of products. The more freedom the individual has to balance money income against the use of his productive capacity to create utility in other forms, the less correspondence there will be be-tween the relative utility and relative cost, of different product units unless workers are free to move from one occupation to another and are homogeneous, and con-ditions are such that they move in response to an insig-nificant difference in money earnings in the two fields.

21. The conception of productive capacity is like many if not most others in the field of interpretation of be-havior, it is indispensable to analysis yet cannot be made precise. To begin with, it is fundamentally ambiguous in meaning, a different thing to buyer and seller. What

the buyer—producer-entrepreneur—wants, and gets, is product, a stream of some specific result-stream. In the abstract, it is simply *value* product, an increment of total money return; anything more specific in connection with the laborer's performance might be said to belong to technology, not economics. But nominally and formally, the production manager bargains for and buys a service marketed and priced under its own specific name. This may be either the "time" of a particular individual worker, or the performance of some physically defined and measured result. In the competitive determination of the payment, we must assume that it is the latter, from the employer's point of view, that all wages are "really" piece wages. But from a general human standpoint, and particularly from that of the worker himself, the payment is compensation for whatever he gives up in order to earn it. The economic theorist must view this choice as one between different uses of capacity to create "utility" in the two quantitatively comparable and hence fundamentally homogeneous groups of "forms", consumption of products bought with money, and other, competing, values.

The objective dimensions of productive capacity are quantity of productive resource, physically defined—where it is continuously divisible—and *time;* where the physical resource in question is an indivisible unit, such as a laborer (or any machine or tool while it exists as a unit) the only effective dimension is time. Capacity in this sense is variously apportioned between different occupations by division of the continuous, chronological time stream, "transversely", at appropriate intervals. The movement of a physical agency from one occupation to another may or may not involve physical transportation of the agency itself; when it does not, the associated rearrangements of the productive process as a whole may be indefinitely various in kind.[19]

But there are other ways of dividing the capacity of an agency between different uses, of splitting the time

[19] See above, Sec. 15, on assumptions regarding cost of movement and speed, or time involved.

use-stream longitudinally in effect,[20] and in a theoretical analysis each such way becomes a dimension of capacity itself. Again, discussion may be practically limited to the case of the human being as a laborer; most of the features have more or less of a parallel in connection with other agencies, but the special problems in other cases are not difficult. The simplest and most nearly objective or physical of the dimensions other than time is that of speed at work. It is to be assumed that the worker will work up into the speed range where increase absorbs capacity for enjoyment in some form, for he is assumed to be paid according to results. If increased speed involves increased fatigue (which it may or may not do), the worker's capacity for creating utility in other forms is reduced. Here another distinction must be made, and the problem of dimensions becomes more subtle. It is one thing to reduce by increased speed of work one's capacity for enjoyment *at other times,* when not at work; it is a different, but obviously a real, thing to vary one's "net enjoyment" while at work. Again, there are other ways of varying both net enjoyment while at work and one's state of fatigue or capacity for other activities or for their enjoyment when not at work. There are also diverse ways to vary the *value* of the results of one's work, besides varying the speed of work. Variation in the quality of performance through variation in effort of attention comes to mind at once, but there is an indefinite list of other ways not so obvious, and it is probably impossible to give a clear general description, still less an exhaustive list of the modes of variation, or the dimensions of productive capacity. Speed of work is, of course, relative to quality, and even where no other variation in quality occurs, the proportion of "spoiled" work affords a continuous variation of average quality.

The phase of the problem of capacity which is most important and most difficult is, however, the phase involved in the choice between occupations affected with

[20] Movements from any of a group of activities or experiences to any other, at frequent intervals, and without cost, amounts in effect to a simultaneous combination of all, proportioned at will. This is the assumption commonly made on the utility side.

different subjective attitudes. The special difficulty, as is usual in such economic problems, is connected with the role of time. The special relative appeal (or "disappeal") of an occupation may be in various degrees a function of the amount of time devoted to it. The degree may be practically zero, as when it is due to the social repute or disrepute attached to the job or to something with which it is inseparably connected, but also when it involves living at some unsatisfactory place or under unsatisfactory social surroundings. There is a superficial element of unreality in viewing the power or potentiality of earning income through suffering relatively unpleasant concomitants as a form of productive capacity; but if subjective factors of any sort, i.e., factors other than the amount of money income earned, influencing the choice of occupations, are to be taken into account, this view is necessary to the rational interpretation of choice.

When the subjective elements in an occupation do not vary with the amount of work done (money earned), the amount will depend on the number of individuals attracted to the occupation by earnings sufficient to overcome this repugnance, as estimated by each, and by their rate of performance as determined by the operation of other factors which do vary with the rate itself. It is an interesting feature of human psychology that the stigma attached to an occupation seems to vary, more or less, inversely with the amount of income it carries with it. A thing which is disreputable, if done in a small or petty way, loses much of this quality if it makes possible an upper-class mode of life. Of course, social stigma is also profoundly affected in very subtle ways by innumerable other factors also; as the proverb says, "it is not what one does, but the way in which one does it" which determines moral rating. This applies to stigmas of various sorts, from dealings of a fraudulent or oppressive character to things disreputable on moral or social grounds. In general, such factors make surprisingly little difference in wage rates, hours worked, or total earnings.

22. Where the relative, subjective appeal of an occupation varies (at the margin, in comparison with alterna-

tives) with the amount of work done, i.e., money earned, and where at the same time the individual has reasonable freedom to vary all three in relation, this factor will naturally be balanced against the alternatives. The simple case, again, is variation by reapportionment of the worker's time stream, the number of "hours" per day or some longer time unit, spent at the task. It seems reasonable to believe that this is the overwhelmingly important mode of variation, for several reasons. The first in importance is the undoubted fact that the value of income in consumption is largely dependent on "free" time. (This principle must not be pressed too far, as there are numerous "bottomless" uses of money income which interfere little or not at all with the distribution of one's time.) In the second place, the degree of freedom open to workers to vary the hourly rate of earnings is restricted, on the whole, though perhaps less so than freedom to vary the "hours" of work. Again, and perhaps more important, the psychological gain through doing less work in a given time is probably restricted in general. If one is going to work at all there is presumably a "natural gait" beyond which one cannot go far without intolerably increasing physical strain and presently reducing proportionally the hours which it is possible to work, while on the other hand there will be little psychic gain in working at a much lower rate than this natural gait; it may even be a positive annoyance and require increased effort of attention to do so. Of course, the natural gait will vary with conditions, increasing as skill is built up either by effort or unconsciously.

No special complication in cost theory will be involved in the fact of subjective preference if conditions are generally such that the difference in subjective quality of the activity of producing a unit of output in any field both can be and will be compensated by producing a different number of units. In that case, the total money income of the worker will always be the same in any occupation into which he may move, or, in other words, a given capacity will always earn the same money income regardless of the occupation in which it is employed. Where at equilibrium any laborers are mobile under this condition some units of output are produced under the principle of alternative product cost and the entire output may be said to have its value determined by that principle. But all units of an output are marginal at a given price only if in part produced by labor (or other productive agents) actually on an indifference margin at the prices of the moment. If this is true of all the productive capacity in the industry, the product will have a constant cost curve. This may be practically true even if some productive agencies used in the industry are specialized, provided the decrease in return with increasing proportions of the mobile agencies with them is slight (freedom of substitution high) in comparison with price flexibility (reciprocal of demand elasticity) in the market for the product.

Finally, it is to be observed that all this intricate theoretical development on the topic of subjective preference, while important for analysis, probably has relatively little importance in practice. It is very doubtful that laborers or owners of other productive agents sacrifice money return for other considerations to any large extent on the whole. The classical theory of noncompeting groups rested on the observation of Mill as well as Cairnes, and indeed of every thoughtful person, that in general it is the people with high money incomes who get the other pleasant perquisites of productive life, that the more disagreeable work pays the lower wages. From another point of view, all observation concurs in the judgment that observed wage differences are mainly traceable to other facts than the relative subjective advantages or disadvantages of the work. It is not true, on the other hand, that labor is in any way or degree homogeneous, or properly to be called a "factor" of production. Laborers above the ranks of the unskilled are typically specialized and their earnings, together with those of capital specialized instruments, are far more typically and purely "rent" than is the return on "land".[21]

[21] This phase of the discussion may be closed with a few notes on the relations between labor and property. For property items there is usually little "sentimental" difference to the owner in connection with any form of variation in the rate of performance

Notes on Utility and Cost

V

23. The relative part played by (relative) cost and (relative) utility in determining price is a matter simply of the relative elasticities of the supply and demand curves. If consumers freely substitute over a wide range a comparatively fixed amount of one commodity for a given amount of another in the apportionment of consumption, the price of these two amounts which replace each other can never be very different, regardless of cost conditions. This will be true if the products are closely similar. If, on the other hand, producers have a high degree of freedom in replacing the production of a given amount of one commodity by the production of a given amount of another through the transfer of resources, these two amounts can never be very different in price, regardless of utility and demand conditions. This will be true if the products are made by the same or closely similar productive resources. Finally, control is a matter of which curve is more elastic in comparison with the other.

The statement commonly made—notably by Marshall, and by other writers following him—that demand conditions control in the short run cost conditions in the long run, rests on the assumption that in the short run demand is elastic in comparison with the supply, while the allowance of longer periods for adjustment increases the elasticity of supply without affecting, or at least without correspondingly increasing, the elasticity of demand. There may well be some truth in this assumption, but it cannot be made in any such sweeping fashion. The outstanding fact is that the elasticity of both demand and supply is very low at a moment, and increases almost indefinitely with the time allowed for the readjustment.

---

in a given occupation. There are sentimental preferences as to occupation, as was noted by both Smith and Ricardo. But it is doubtful whether these make a large difference in rates of earnings. The difference is surprisingly little in the case of labor, and people who will not put their property into disreputable uses generally feel free to sell it to others, at least to dealers, without reservation as to use.

Notes on Utility and Cost

It is to be remembered that the existence of stocks of ordinary consumption goods presumably held for speculative purposes provides for a degree of flexibility of supply within intervals too short for transfer of production.

Serious embarrassment arises from the fact that there is no conceivable way of determining the elasticity of either demand or supply with reference to any particular time period. The statistical methods available for getting an idea of actual elasticities in a fairly definite region of time and place, depend on the spontaneous uncontrolled occurrence of comparatively quick changes on one side of the relation, without corresponding changes on the other. Sudden changes in demand against constant productive conditions may yield an approximate supply curve, sudden changes in supply against an assumed constancy of demand, an approximate demand curve; and the approximation is at best not close. What the amount and speed of change in either amount consumed or amount produced, resulting from a given price change, would be, with conditions held constant but time allowed for approximation to an equilibrium adjustment, must apparently remain a matter for estimate from very general considerations or extremely indirect calculation. For this there is, of course, the further conclusive reason that the conditions underlying either curve will never actually remain constant while any adjustment to equilibrium is working itself out.

As to the chance of making any estimate or calculation of elasticity for any real period, the possibilities in the abstract are limited enough on the supply side, but are virtually zero on that of demand. The willingness of consumers to make substitutions is determined by facts of social psychology, which are created and constantly recreated by historical process, more or less influenced by the planned activities of individuals, business enterprises, and governments (advertising, education), but of the underlying forces, in a quantitative sense, there seems little prospect of securing any definite knowledge. The one thing we can say with conviction is that flexibility under given conditions is a matter of time; and that the assumption common in economic literature that the demand curve is an instantaneous expression of basic demand conditions not subject to lag in adjustment when there is a change in either variable is certainly false to the facts.

On the supply side, it is at least possible to give some analysis of the problem, to list a number of distinct factors or conditions, more or less ascertainable, which affect the flexibility of supply. The primary consideration is, of course, the fluidity or mobility of the agencies of production. This, again, breaks down into two great groups, the human and the material factors. Again, there is a breakdown on the human side, between natural ability and training. On the side of non-human agencies we also find two separable sets of considerations, the degree of specificity in the suitability of individual instruments as they exist at any time, as against their freedom of replacement, depending in the first place on length of life, or, reciprocally, rate of turnover. From another standpoint, the whole situation involves three main elements. The first is the amount of difference in the productive agencies used in different fields at a given time, including (a) physical suitability and (b) owner's preference as to use. The second is the resistance to change in the adaptive qualities of agencies, (a) as existing things (remodelling or retraining), or (b) through replacement by different kinds. The third is the flexibility of proportions in technical combination between relatively specialized and relatively mobile agencies; the steeper the curve of "diminishing (physical) returns" from the relatively mobile as they are applied in varying proportions to the relatively more specialized, the lower will be the elasticity of supply.

Opinions differ widely as to the facts. A general knowledge of technical conditions in industry seems to the writer to point clearly in the direction of a very high degree of elasticity if a moderate length of time is allowed for adjustment, as regards the field of industry as a whole; there are, of course, numerous exceptions, of varying importance. Here, again, fundamental conditions cannot be assumed to remain fixed; it is apparently a psychological fact that a rapid rise in the price of any product to a point conspicuously above accustomed levels operates as a stimulus to research and experiment in the use of resources in producing it, which almost always leads to "historical" changes [22] moving its relative cost curve downward.

In conclusion we may suggest that a part of the confusion between "opportunity" or "displacement" costs and "real" costs is due to bad terminology. All cost which affects supply and price is resource cost and all resource cost is alternative cost. "Rents" are not costs at all, but the extreme ambiguity and general misuse of this conception must be watched for as a constant source of confusion. There is an important difference in kinds of price determining cost based on the character of the alternative use of resources which makes it necessary that a product bring a price which will remunerate them at a given level as a condition of their being used to produce it. The next best alternative may be use to produce some other salable product or use to create utility for the owner of the resource in "non-pecuniary" form.[23] If it is thought desirable to have names descriptive of the-

[22] Such historical changes should *not* be referred to as "dynamic". If terms taken from mechanics are to be used in economics, they should be used in something like their original meaning. Economic dynamics will then deal with the relations between force and resistance in connection with changes under given fundamental conditions. In any case, there must be some clear distinction between this field of investigation and that dealing with changes in the basic economic data. To this "historical" field, there is no analogy in mechanics, at least not within the limits in which the "Newtonian" conceptions are applicable, and these seem to hold out to far more decimal places than the economist can ever hope to fill.

[23] For some problems, notably in the field of money, it is more useful to distinguish between products actually entering into commerce and those which do not, even if the latter are economically identical with and displace the former. It would not be possible to draw with empirical definiteness the line between the marketable and the non-marketable. The distinction between what is and what is not marketed is an objective one, but is less significant than the other. (Cf. above, pp. 5, 25.)

oretical differences the two types of cost might be called "relative" and "absolute" cost or perhaps alternative product cost and non-monetary alternative cost, both being carefully distinguished from price-determined cost, or rent. Surely the form of exposition should in some way make prominent the difference between money costs which express and measure "real" costs affecting any unit of a *product* and which can be compared as between one *product* and another, and money costs which relate only to a particular product but which are still "real" in that they mediate a sacrificed alternative and affect supply and price.

CPSIA information can be obtained
at www.ICGtesting.com
Printed in the USA
LVHW090838130120
643295LV00004B/6/P